NELSON Language ARTS

MAKING A DIFFERENCE

Gerald Best

Caren Cameron

Maureen Dockendorf

Barb Eklund

Christine Finochio

Ruth Hay

Sharon Jeroski

Eugene Mazur

Mary McCarthy

Maureen Skinner

Senior Program Consultant

Jennette MacKenzie

I(T)P Nelson

an International Thomson Publishing company

Toronto • Albany • Bonn • Boston • Cincinnati • Detroit • London • Madrid • Melbourne
Mexico City • New York • Pacific Grove • Paris • San Francisco • Singapore • Tokyo • Washington

Grade 5 Reviewers:

Lynn Archer
New Westminster, British Columbia

Faye Brownbridge
Calgary, Alberta

Caren Cameron
Victoria, British Columbia

Katherine Collis
Winnipeg, Manitoba

Dr. Elaine Crocker
St. John's, Newfoundland

Diana Cruise
Winnipeg, Manitoba

Wendy Davidson
Truro, Nova Scotia

Ann Dominick
North York, Ontario

Nancy Farrell
Burnaby, British Columbia

Irene Heffel
Edmonton, Alberta

Helen Hohmann
Edmonton, Alberta

Nancy Leonard
Markham, Ontario

Patti Peroni
Brampton, Ontario

Equity Consultant:
Ken Ramphal

I(T)P® International Thomson Publishing
The ITP logo is a trademark under licence
www.thomson.com

Published by
I(T)P® Nelson
A division of Thomson Canada Limited, 1998
1120 Birchmount Road
Scarborough, Ontario M1K 5G4
www.nelson.com

Printed and bound in Canada
5 6 7 8 9 0 / ITIB / 7 6 5 4

Canadian Cataloguing in Publication Data

Main entry under title:

Nelson language arts 5

ISBN 0-17-607526-7 (v. 2 : bound)
ISBN 0-17-607429-5 (v. 2 : pbk.)
Contents: [2] Making a Difference

1. Readers (Elementary). I. Cameron, Caren, 1949–

PE1121.N448 1997   428.6   C97-931515-8

Project Team: Angela Cluer, Mark Cobham, Kathleen ffolliott, Vicki Gould, Susan Green, Ann Ludbrook, John McInnes, Marcia Miron, June Reynolds, Theresa Thomas, Jill Young

Art Direction and Production: Liz Harasymczuk

TABLE OF CONTENTS

Unit 1 *Making a Difference*   6

We Are Plooters   8
by Jack Prelutsky *(poem)*

The Last Days of the Giddywit   10
by Natalie Babbitt *(short story)*

A Landfill Debate in New Brunswick   16
by Susan Green *(information article)*

The Earth Game   18
by Pam Conrad *(short story)*

The Lightwell   22
by Laurence Yep *(short story)*

The Visitor   24
by Elizabeth Brochmann *(short story)*

The Vision Seeker   28
by James Whetung *(legend)*

Sweet Clara and the Freedom Quilt   36
by Deborah Hopkinson *(narrative fiction)*

Awards Day   46
by Ann Rivkin *(narrative fiction)*

Working Together with One Heart   56
by Todd Mercer *(articles)*
   The Arctic Winter Games   57
   Jesse Ketchum Pan Vibrations   59

With Two Wings   62
by Red and Kathy Grammer *(song lyrics)*

Unit Wrap-up   64

Unit 2 *All About Structures*   68

Natural Builders   70
by Susan Green *(photo essay)*

Meet the Architects   74
by Todd Mercer *(interviews and profile)*
    Kim Storey   75
    Douglas Cardinal   80
    Frank Gehry   82

How to Build a House   84
by Trudee Romanek *(information text and diagrams)*

Make a Model Room   96
by John Williams *(instructions)*

The Little Pigs Housing Project   100
by John McInnes *(cartoon story)*

Bridges   108
by Trudee Romanek
    Confederation Bridge 110
    (information text and diagrams)
    Other Famous Canadian Bridges 114
    (information text)

I Was Born Here in This City   116
by Arnold Adoff *(poem)*

Unit Wrap-up   118

Unit 3 *In This Place*   122

Canada, My Home   124
(poetry, prose, and illustrations)

The Dip   130
by Jan Andrews *(short story)*

Naomi's Road   **136**
by Joy Kogawa *(novel excerpt)*

Josepha: A Prairie Boy's Story   **142**
by Jim McGugan *(narrative fiction)*

In My Back Yard   **152**
(haiku)

The First Red Maple Leaf   **154**
by Ludmila Zeman *(legend)*

Akla Gives Chase   **158**
by James Houston *(narrative fiction)*

Picture This   **170**
    In the Wet Haze   **170**
    by Patrick Lane *(poem)*
    I Am   **171**
    by Marilyn Helmer *(poem)*
    January in Suburban Windsor   **171**
    by Tom Wayman *(poem)*
    pender street east   **172**
    by Jim Wong-Chu *(poem)*
    Ice   **172**
    by Gary Geddes *(poem)*
    River   **173**
    by Archie Toulouse *(poem)*
    And my heart soars   **174**
    by Chief Dan George *(poem)*
    rush hour in the rain   **175**
    by Tiffany Stone *(poem)*

An Adventure on Island Rock   **176**
by L. M. Montgomery *(narrative fiction)*

Unit Wrap-up   **186**

Unit 1: *Making a Difference*

You are constantly affected by the people and events around you. At the same time, you yourself affect those same people and events. Have you ever thought "What can *I* do to make a difference?" In this unit, you will read stories and poems about people who have chosen to make a difference to their friends, their family, their community, and their world. As you read and discuss different issues, you will learn how you can make a difference by working together, solving problems, thinking about the consequences of your actions, being a good listener, and supporting others. You will

- read how other people made a difference to their world
- look at how one person's decisions can affect many people
- understand that you can make a difference
- learn new reading strategies to help you understand the meaning of what you read
- work together in a group to share responsibility and to support one another
- create a plan to make a difference

6

7

We Are Plooters

Written by Jack Prelutsky
Illustrated by Sean Dawdy

READING TIP

Set a purpose for reading

Poems can give us important messages. Look at both the title of the poem and the illustration. Before you read, predict what message the poem will have for you.

We are Plooters,
We don't care,
We make messes
Everywhere,
We strip forests
Bare of trees,
We dump garbage
In the seas.
    We are Plooters,
    We enjoy
    Finding beauty
    To destroy,

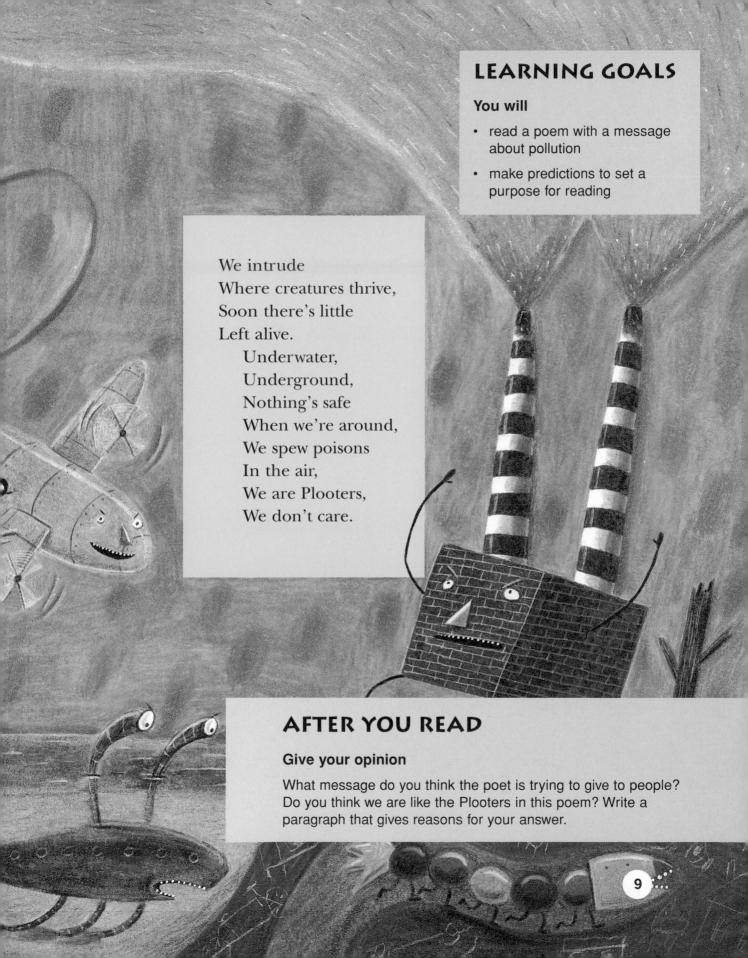

We intrude
Where creatures thrive,
Soon there's little
Left alive.
　Underwater,
　Underground,
　Nothing's safe
When we're around,
We spew poisons
In the air,
We are Plooters,
We don't care.

AFTER YOU READ

Give your opinion

What message do you think the poet is trying to give to people?
Do you think we are like the Plooters in this poem? Write a
paragraph that gives reasons for your answer.

The Last Days
of the
GIDDYWIT

Written by Natalie Babbitt
Illustrated by Steven Kellogg

READING TIP

Think about what you know

Make a list of all the ways you use to get rid of your garbage.
Think about what people from a long time ago might have
done with their garbage. Read to find out how they might
have solved their garbage problem.

Years and years ago, in the time when houses were caves—this was after the dinosaurs but a while before shovels—there was a tribe of people called the Giddywit. They lived all together, and every day the men would go out and hunt supper while the women stayed home to pick nuts and berries and teach the babies how to swat flies. Then at night, when the men came back, everyone would feast on mammoth meat or reindeer, with a side of the nuts and berries, and they tossed the garbage in a corner.

A Giddywit battling a fly.

After a few weeks, of course, the pile of garbage would get pretty big and smelly, and the flies were something fierce, so the Giddywit would pack up their furs and clubs, and the babies' bibs and swatters, and move to a new cave. This always caused great confusion, with snarling and arguments, and once in a while a baby would get left behind and have to be fetched. But soon the Giddywit would be settled again in a nice fresh place and could start over, tossing garbage and swatting flies.

Now, there was among the Giddywit a thin little man named Oog who wasn't allowed to hunt mammoths because he only got in the way. So his job was to look for eggs. He was good at climbing trees, way up where the nests were, and while he was up there, he would look out over the land where everything was wild and sweet and didn't ever seem to get smelly. "This is nice," he would say to himself. "I wish *we*

11

could live in trees." But they couldn't because of having to hang on, even while sound asleep, which would have been hard for everyone, especially the babies. Still, Oog thought a lot about how nice it was, far away from the garbage.

One night in the cave—it was summer, and the flies and the garbage were atrocious—Oog said to everyone, "Why don't we try putting the garbage outside?"

"Outside?" said everyone. "You're a dope, Oog. If you want to bring every bear and tiger in the neighbourhood nosing around the door, that's the way to do it." And they snickered at Oog and poked each other with their elbows and winked.

"We could dig holes and bury the garbage, maybe," said Oog.

"Who's got time to dig holes?" they said, with more snickers and winks. "Sure, if we had a shovel. But it's still a while before shovels. And anyway, what's wrong with moving to a new cave?"

Oog Dreaming

"We might run out of caves," said Oog.

"Run out of caves!" they cried. "You're a dope, Oog." And they winked and poked each other again and threw more garbage in a corner, and then they lay down on their furs and went to sleep.

But Oog sat up, swatting flies, and thought it over. And the next morning, instead of climbing trees to look for eggs, he took

Mrs. Oog by the hand and went away, a long way off, miles and miles through the wild, sweet land, and came after many days to a little cave just right for two. "This is the ticket," he said to Mrs. Oog. "We'll live on nuts and berries and the very occasional rabbit, and of course we'll always have eggs. And we'll never throw garbage into corners."

"But, dear," said Mrs. Oog, "what will we *do* with the garbage? We'll have to put it *some*where."

"We'll bury it," said Oog.

"But, dear," said Mrs. Oog, "we can't do that without shovels to dig the holes."

"We won't need very big holes," said Oog. "Not with only two. So I shall invent the spoon and dig with that."

"Clever," said Mrs. Oog. "And I shall invent the fork. To keep our fingers clean at supper. It's time."

So Oog and Mrs. Oog invented the spoon and fork and buried their garbage outside the cave, and everything stayed nice and clean, and they were happy as clams even though they'd never seen a clam, until one day, a year or so later, here came the rest of the Giddywit, tramping along with their furs and babies, arguing and snarling.

"Well, well," said Oog. "What brings the lot of you to *these* far parts?"

"We ran out of caves," said everyone. "And now you're going to snicker, aren't you?"

"No," said Oog, "but maybe you've learned that you have to bury your garbage."

"Can't do it," said everyone. "It's still too long before shovels."

"Maybe so," said Oog, "but I've invented the spoon, which is pretty good for digging."

"Oog," they said, "you're still a dope. Digging with a—what did you call it? A spoon?—is too much work for the kind of hole *we'd* need. We'll just go on and look for another bunch of caves."

So they did, still snarling and arguing, and Oog never saw them again, except, as it happens, for the babies. For the Giddywit found a new cave farther on and settled down to tossing and swatting. And then one night, when the wind was in the right direction, some bears and tigers sniffed out the cave and finished off the Giddywit, except for the babies, and left no garbage at all. The babies found their way back to Oog and Mrs. Oog, who, having no babies of their own, were delighted. And Oog made a great big spoon to dig holes with, so that shovels were invented at last, because what is a shovel but a great big spoon?

Mr. and Mrs. Oog teaching the baby Giddywits.

So that was the end of the Giddywit and the start of the Oogites, a neat and tidy tribe from which we are all descended.

Maybe.

AFTER YOU READ

Draw conclusions

What method of waste disposal did Oog invent? Make a list of the advantages and disadvantages of this system. In what other ways might the Giddywit dispose of their garbage?

A Landfill Debate in

NEW BRUNSWICK

Written by Susan Green

READING TIP

Ask questions

Imagine that your community has no more room to dump its garbage and a possible solution might be to bury the garbage in a landfill site. What questions would you want answered before you agreed that this would be a good decision? Read to find answers to your questions.

For several years, the New Brunswick government has been searching for new landfill sites for dumping garbage. A site at Crane Mountain in Saint John was chosen in 1997.

However, not everyone in the province agrees with the decision to use Crane Mountain. Many people in the communities around Saint John are concerned.

Wednesday, February 5, 1997
Saint John Times Globe
Landfill Will Go Ahead

Monday, February 10, 1997
Saint John Times Globe
Risks at Crane Shouldn't Be Ignored

Here are several of the reasons for and reasons against using the Crane Mountain landfill site.

Reasons For	Reasons Against
• safety precautions in place	• close to populated areas
• 41% of trash can be recycled instead of sending it to a landfill	• leaks will pollute drinking water and possibly cause health problems
• the landfill's design will minimize pollution	• eyesore for tourists driving on highway between Saint John and Fredericton
• studies will be done on the site to ensure minimal risks	• traffic danger because of the number of garbage trucks
• the site will be regularly tested for signs of pollution	• cost to taxpayers (over $11 million)

New Brunswickers continue to talk about what Crane Mountain will do to the environment. It is a reminder to all Canadians that the decisions we make today about what to do with garbage will affect the future of the land and the people who will live there.

AFTER YOU READ

Make a decision

In your notebook, make a chart like the one below that shows the positive and negative sides to this issue. Find information for both columns. Examine the information. Based on this evidence, what would you do?

Positive/Pro Side	Negative/Con Side

T·H·E
Earth Game

Written by Pam Conrad
Illustrated by Odile Ouellet

READING TIP

Think about your experiences

Think about a decision you once made that had negative consequences for other people and a decision that had positive consequences. Draw a web to show how your decision affected other people. Read how decisions made about our environment can affect everyone.

Not very long ago, in a meadow not too far from here, some children found a ball of twine lying in the grass.

"Watch me," called the oldest girl. And she tied the end of the string to her finger and tossed the ball in the air.

Her brother caught it and wrapped the string around his own finger. Then he pitched it across to his friend. The twine unwound just enough as it sailed through the air. His friend caught the ball, wrapped the string around his thumb, and threw it over to someone else.

After many tosses back and forth, the ball had unwound to just a loose end, and the smallest child wound that around his finger. And there they were, joined in a circle by the twine that wove a net at their centre.

"Now look," said the oldest girl, and she wiggled her finger.

"I felt that!" said her brother.

"So did I," said his friend.

And standing very still, one by one, they each wiggled a finger until they could feel the twine move with even the gentlest tug.

"Now, let's be the Earth," said the girl. She closed her eyes, and her voice lifted over the meadow. "I am a jungle in Africa, and someone is shooting an elephant for his tusks." She moved her finger. They all felt the tug and grew sad.

"I'm the Arctic Ocean," said her brother, "and an oil tanker is hitting an iceberg and spilling oil over me. Soon all

the birds will be black and slick and won't fly anymore." He tugged, and they were silent.

"I am a big city, and no one can see the stars in the sky because the air is thick with smoke and fumes from my factories." The gentle tug passed around them.

"I was once a farm, but the sunflowers and rows of corn are gone. Today I am a mall." They each felt the sad tug.

They stopped tugging. It was as though a thick cloud had passed before the sun and darkened their day. It was very still, except for a bird whizzing by over their heads.

Then the smallest boy smiled. He moved his finger. "I'm a town, and in a back yard somebody's putting out seed for the winter birds." He tugged again, and their faces lit up.

"Yes!" The tallest girl raised her hands, and the pull was felt by all. "I'm a highway, and people are walking alongside me, picking up bottles and cans for recycling." She wiggled her fingers and laughed, and they could all feel it.

"I'm a neighbourhood, and people are planting trees along my concrete sidewalks."

"I am an ocean, and fishermen are freeing the dolphins from their nets."

"I'm a herd of wild mustangs, and someone has given me land and turned me loose."

"I'm a lonely country road, and somebody's painting my mailbox red."

They all laughed. Then they raised their hands, lifting the net of twine higher and higher. They could feel the certain pull of all the things people could do to make a better world.

And that is how—not too long ago, in a meadow not very far from here—a ball of twine was the beginning of the Earth game.

AFTER YOU READ

Make connections

Reread the story and pick one decision or event that had a positive consequence and one that had a negative consequence. Make a chart or web to show how that choice or event affected others. What decisions can you make about your environment that will make a difference to your community or the world?

The Lightwell

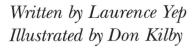

Written by *Laurence Yep*
Illustrated by *Don Kilby*

READING TIP

Think like an author

Authors often use descriptive language to make their readers
feel as if they were actually in the story. As you read this
story, look for words that make you feel as if you were in the
grandmother's apartment.

My grandmother lives in a tiny studio apartment in
Chinatown. Her home, in the rear of the building, receives
no direct sunlight even though her window opens on a
lightwell; for the lightwell seems to stretch endlessly upward
and downward among the many buildings. At its brightest, it
is filled with a kind of tired twilight.

Although the lightwell is a poor source for light, it is a
perfect carrier for sound. In the mornings it carries sound
from all the other apartments—the slap of wet laundry being
hung in a window, the rush of water into a sink, the crying of
a baby. During the afternoons, bits of conversation float into
my grandmother's home like fragments of little dramas and
comedies—just as, I'm sure, the other tenants can hear the

shuffling of my grandmother's cards and her exclamations when she loses at solitaire.

Toward evening, as my grandmother clanks pots on her stove, I can hear matching sounds from the other apartments as her neighbours also prepare their meals. And the smell of my grandmother's simmering rice and frying vegetables mingles with the other smells in the lightwell until there are enough aromas for a banquet.

Side by side, top and below, each of us lives in our own separate time and space. And yet we all belong to the same building, our lives touching however briefly and faintly.

AFTER YOU READ

Use descriptive language

Draw a picture of where you live. Around your picture, add words and phrases that describe the sounds and smells of your home. Do the words make your readers feel as if they were actually there?

⚹ The Visitor ⚹

Written by Elizabeth Brochmann
Illustrated by Carmelo Blandino

READING TIP

Think of your experiences

Think about a time when you did something, not because you wanted to but because you did not want to hurt someone else's feelings. How did you feel? Compare your feelings with those of the writer of this story.

I am the visitor. Mr. Boyd is blind, and Mrs. Boyd waves me to come over the fence and visit him. I don't want to go anymore. I used to want to go often. But now I often don't want to go.

Obediently I climb the fence and follow her into the living room to wait for Mr. Boyd to come out of the bedroom.

Mrs. Boyd serves me sweet preserves and tiny cakes made with icing faces just to please me. But I am too old for cakes with faces. Meanwhile Mr. Boyd comes into the room. He has braided me another tassel out of five wheat stems. All the while he smiles and asks me questions. The same questions. He ties a ribbon on his good luck charms just to please me. But I am too grown for the same questions or the

24

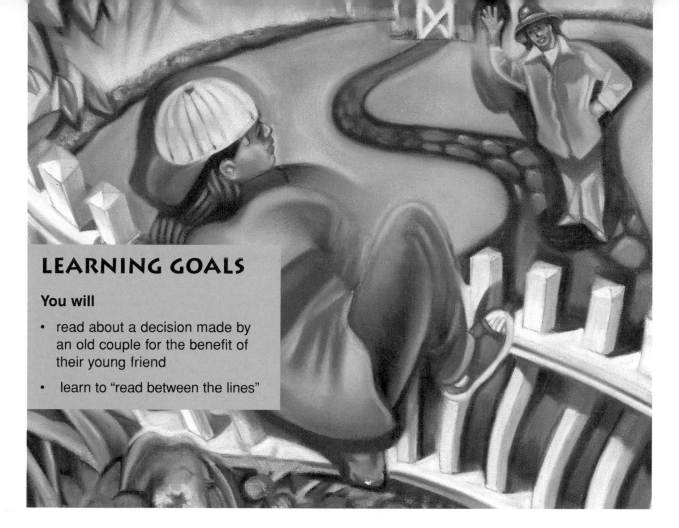

ribbon or the charms. I do not want to hurt them. I want to be off by myself, thinking and reading. Or playing with friends. I want to be off.

Mrs. Boyd pours my tea. I used to beg to come over, nag to come over, until finally Mom would sigh and let me climb the fence again—but with a warning. "You'll wear out your welcome." But I never did. They were always happy to have me.

I don't want them to be sad, Mr. and Mrs. Boyd. I don't want to tell them, "I want to be off alone." Mrs. Boyd spoons sweet pie cherries into my bowl.

"How's the fishing?" Mr. Boyd asks. The fish in the river are too small for me to catch now. It's no longer a thrill to catch them.

Mrs. Boyd serves Mr. Boyd, and she pushes the spoon along the tablecloth so he can find it. "How's that scarf you're knitting coming along?" Scarf? Finished or thrown aside a long time ago—I can't remember how long ago—when I was little. I don't care about knitting now.

I can't tell them how much I want to be off.

"Ahhhm," Mrs. Boyd clears her throat as she serves herself the last of the cherries last of all. "Mr. Boyd and I, we called you over for a reason today. We want to tell you something." Mr. Boyd stares at the back of his spoon as if he might see himself there. "Yes, Mr. Boyd and I have been talking. We figure it's time. Sad to say, but it's about how busy we're getting these days."

I look at her.

"Yes," says Mr. Boyd. "Very busy."

I look at him.

"I'm getting busier and busier braiding my tassels." Tassels hang from every corner of every room. "Take a few to your friends." The house is festooned with them, tacked to doorways and pinned on curtains and on the picture calendars, each tied with a ribbon. Mr. Boyd never seems to tire of making them, and Mrs. Boyd never seems to tire of hanging them up. In that way they are not like me. Mr. Boyd polishes his spoon. "And Mrs. Boyd, she's busy looking after me." He grins and winks at me over the teapot that looks like a cottage with a straw roof.

"And we were wondering," said Mrs. Boyd, "if you could come over perhaps only once every month or two?"

I forget to eat, and the cherries spill off my spoon— plop, plop into my dish. "It's not that we won't miss you, but we are getting terribly busy these days, and I suspect you are too."

"Don't worry." Mr. Boyd finds my hand, squeezes it. "It's not goodbye forever." And Mrs. Boyd squeezes my other hand with the spoon still in it. "No, don't worry. We won't forget you. And you won't forget us."

I cannot believe this has happened. I look at them smiling at me.

Some day when I am grown up and Mr. and Mrs. Boyd are very, very old, I will send a taxi for them, and I will wait at my gate with my little girl to welcome them.

AFTER YOU READ

Read between the lines

The old couple seemed to know that the girl did not want to visit them anymore, but they never actually said so. When you read a story like this, you have to "read between the lines" to figure out what is happening. Find information in the story that gives you clues that the old couple knew how their young friend was feeling.

The Vision Seeker

Written by James Whetung
Illustrated by Paul Morin

The boy in this story goes to a sweat lodge. This is a dome built of saplings and covered with canvas. The dome is 2.4 m from side to side and only 1.2 m high. It is a place the Anishinaabe and other Aboriginal people used when they needed to think about their lives and the world around them.

Boozhoo. Greetings, original people.

My spirit name is Spirit Bird. My mother's clan is, of common knowledge, Otter. My father says his clan is Black Duck; others say it is Cormorant.

We are continuing our celebration of Anishinaabe life as we gather outside this Sweat Lodge. I will guide you through the teaching of how the Anishinaabe people received the original Sweat Lodge.

LEARNING GOALS

You will

- read a legend about a boy who helps his people by going on a vision quest

- use clues to figure out new words

29

Long ago, there was a period of great darkness. Families feuded within families. Neighbours disagreed with neighbours. Whole communities were in conflict. Entire nations fought with each other.

Everywhere men used their pipes and drums for war, for gaining more land. As I said, it was a very dark time.

The men were so busy making war that none of them had time to hunt. Everyone grew weaker, and then they grew hungrier. It is said they were so weak that they would trip over a twig or even a blade of grass. Some fell and broke their bones. Others simply fell and died. That's how weak the people had become.

A Little Boy, anxious to help his people, asked his parents what he could do. They told him he could go, go to the high place and seek a vision. Maybe through his fast and the Vision Quest he would learn how to help his people.

The Boy's family helped him to get ready. When he was prepared, his grandmothers, his grandfathers, his aunties and uncles, his mother and father, his brothers and sisters— all of them gathered together to wish the Boy well.

Before he left, his mother and father gave him four kernels of corn.

At sunrise on the first day, the Boy began to walk as far as he could to the East. When the sun set, he knew that he had reached his resting place. So he stopped and ate the first kernel of corn.

On the second day, he started walking to the South. He travelled all day, as far as he could. At sunset he knew he was, once again, at his resting place. So he stopped and ate the second kernel of corn.

The next day was the third day, and the Boy set out at dawn once more. He walked all that long day to the West. And once again, when the sun passed through the Western Doorway, he rested and ate the third kernel of corn.

31

On the fourth day, the Boy rose at sunrise and walked North until sundown. Finally, he ate the fourth, last kernel of corn.

The Boy had reached the high place, the place where he would seek his vision. And so he rested and began to fast. It is not known how long he went without food and water, but by and by, the Boy began to dream.

In one of his dreams, he travelled through the four levels of colour, to the dark side of the moon. When he arrived, he saw a lodge, and inside the lodge he could hear voices. The Little Boy was afraid and shy. But then, a friendly voice called from within.

"So, you are the Vision Seeker. Come inside, you are welcome. There is nothing to fear."

The Little Boy stepped forward and entered the lodge.

A wooden vessel was before the Seven Grandfathers. One by one, they dipped their fingers into it and rubbed water on the child. By doing this, each Grandfather gave the Vision Seeker a gift.

The Eastern Grandfather gave him knowledge. The Southern Grandfather gave him love. The Western Grandfather gave honesty. The Northern Grandfather gave strength. The Above Grandfather gave the Boy bravery. The Centre Grandfather gave respect and the Below Grandfather gave him humility.

Then the Seven Grandfathers instructed the Boy to look into the water in the bottom of the vessel. All of creation was flashing into the Boy's eyes. The sight was so overwhelming that he had to look away. But he had seen enough to receive the sacred instructions. He understood

that he must share his vision with his people if they were to
survive. The Grandfathers told him it was time to return to
the high place.

When the Boy awoke, he was lying, weak and hungry
and thirsty, on the ground of the high place. He reached
out and picked a little piece of green cedar bough and ate
it. With that cedar he broke his fast.

The Boy lay still, trying to remember what he was supposed to do. When he was stronger, he sat up and felt the warmth of sunrise on his back. As he looked down from that high place toward his village, he saw a fire. In the fire he saw the Seven Grandfathers. Then he remembered his vision and the gifts he received from those Grandfathers, the gifts he must share with his people.

The Boy's shadow, cast by the rising sun, fell across the mountain, across the fire, and through the opening on a doorway of a dwelling lodge. And the people waiting there stirred.

The Vision Seeker had come home.

Inside there were Seven Grandfathers with long, flowing, white hair. Each and every one of those Grandfathers wore his hair in a different manner.

That lodge was built very much like this one. The cedar trail you see there symbolizes the Boy's shadow. The cedar trail leading to the doorway of this Sweat Lodge symbolizes our connection to our past. The cedar road represents our people joining hands back in time to the origins of this teaching. And that mound you see—that crescent-shaped mound with the cedar placed along the top—represents the high place, the place where visions live. The place that is the dark side of the moon.

Miigwetch.

AFTER YOU READ

Find evidence

Make a list of new words from the story. Beside each word, write the clue you found that helped you to figure out what that word means.

Sweet Clara and the Freedom Quilt

Written by Deborah Hopkinson
Excerpted from the book Sweet Clara and the Freedom Quilt
Illustrated by James Ransome

READING TIP

Identify with the character

Think about a time when you wanted to do something to help someone else, even though you knew it would be difficult for you. How did you try to make it happen? Read to see how the main character in this story tried to help others, in spite of the risks.

Before she's even 12 years old, Clara is taken from North Farm and her mother to work in the fields at the Home Plantation. There she meets other slaves, including a field hand named Young Jack and Aunt Rachel, a woman who takes care of Clara and works sewing in the plantation master's house. Field work is hard for Clara, so Aunt Rachel teaches Clara to be a seamstress so that she too might work in the Big House—that is, if the plantation owner's wife likes Clara's sewing.

The morning sun was streamin' into the sewin' room, turning everything all sunflower yellow. Aunt Rachel give me some sheets to hem. Instead of being contrary, that needle did all I wanted, just like it was part of my hand.

At the end of the day, Missus come in. "Let me see your work, Clara," she say.

I gave her the sheet, and she ran it through her hands real slow. I held my breath, watching.

"From now on, come here," she say at last.

When she left, Aunt Rachel and I looked at each other, about ready to burst. "We done it, girl!" she cried.

So I changed from a field hand to a seamstress. Since the sewin' room was right off the kitchen, Aunt Rachel and I were near Cook and the helpers. There was always lots of bustle and company in the kitchen. I was hearing about all kinds of new places and things. I listened so hard it felt like my ears must be growing out of my head and gettin' big with listening.

One day two white men come to see the master. The drivers went into the kitchen to talk to Cook.

"There been too many runaways last summer," one of the drivers said. "They goin' round askin' all the masters in the county to join the paterollers."

"Crazy, runnin' away," muttered Cook as she beat up some batter. "Where you gon' get to 'cept lost in the swamp?"

"Dunno," said the other. "But I hear we aine that far from the Ohio River. Once you get that far, the Underground Railroad will carry you across."

"That's right," agreed the first. "The Railroad will get you all the way to Canada. Then you free forever."

Cook snorted. "If it be as easy as you two let on, more woulda gone."

One of the men replied in a quiet voice, "It be easy if you could get a map."

Walking back from the Big House that evening I asked Aunt Rachel 'bout what I'd heard. "Where's Canada? And what's the Underground Railroad?"

"See there?" Aunt Rachel pointed. "That's the North Star. Under that star, far up north, is Canada. The Underground Railroad is people who been helpin' folks get there, secret-like."

She looked at me hard. "But don't you start thinkin' 'bout it. You run away and get caught, you be beaten."

Still, I couldn't *stop* thinking about it. Next day I asked Cook, "Those two men that was here yesterday. They was talking 'bout a map. What's a map?"

"Just a picture of the land, that's all. Whatever's on the ground, a map can have it."

Sunday I went to my favourite place on the little hill and looked out at the people's cabins and the fields. I took

a stick and started making a picture in the dirt of all I could see.

But how could I make a picture of things far away that I *couldn't* see? And how could I make a map that wouldn't be washed away by the rain—a map that would show the way to freedom?

Then one day I was sewin' a patch on a pretty blue blanket. The patch looked just the same shape as the cow pond near the cabins. The little stitches looked like a path going all round it. Here it was—a picture that wouldn't wash away. A map!

So I started the quilt.

When you sewin', no matter how careful you be, little scraps of cloth always be left after you cut out a dress or a pillowcase. So while my ears kept listening, and my hands kept sewin', I began to squirrel away these bits of cloth.

When we was off work, I went to visit people in the Quarters. I started askin' what fields was where. Then I started piecin' the scraps of cloth with the scraps of things I was learnin'.

Aunt Rachel say, "Sweet Clara, what kind of pattern you makin' in that quilt? Aine no pattern I ever seen."

"I don't know, Aunt Rachel. I'm just patchin' it together as I go." She looked at me long, but she just nodded.

There was a buzzing in the Quarters one summer evening. I saw the paterollers and I knew someone had run away. It was Young Jack. But five days later they caught him.

That next Sunday I went to see him, and we walked to the top of the little hill. He didn't smile the way he used to.

I took a stick and began to draw in the dirt. I drew a little square for Big House, a line of boxes for the cabins of the Quarters, and some bigger squares for the fields east of Big House. I drew as much as I'd pieced together.

Jack sat beside me, not sayin' anything. Not even looking at first. Then he started seeing what I was doing. I handed the stick to him. I hear him catch his breath up quick. Then he begun to draw.

I worked on the quilt for a long time. Sometimes months would go by and I wouldn't get any pieces sewn in it. Sometimes I had to wait to get the right kind of cloth—I had blue calico and flowered blue silk for creeks and rivers, and greens and blue-greens for the fields, and white sheeting for roads. Missus liked to wear pink a lot, so Big House, the Quarters, and finally, the Big House at North Farm, they was all pink.

The quilt got bigger and bigger, and if folks knew what I was doin', no one said. But they came by the sewin' room to pass the time of day whenever they could.

40

"By the way, Clara," a driver might tell me, "I heard the master sayin' yesterday he didn't want to travel to Mr. Morse's place 'cause it's over twenty miles north o' here."

Or someone would sit eatin' Cook's food and say, so as I could hear, "Word is they gon' plant corn in the three west fields on the Verona plantation this year."

When the master went out huntin', Cook's husband was the guide. He come back and say, "That swamp next to Home Plantation is a nasty place. But listen up, Clara, and I'll tell you how I thread my way in and out of there as smooth as yo' needle in that cloth."

Then one night the quilt was done. I looked at it spread out in the dim light of the cabin. Aunt Rachel studied it for the longest time. She touched the stitches lightly, her fingers moving slowly over the last piece I'd added—a hidden boat that would carry us across the Ohio River. Finally, they came to rest on the bright star at the top.

She tried to make her voice cheery. "You always did like to make patterns and pictures, Clara. You get yourself married to Young Jack one of these days, and you two will have a real nice quilt to sleep under."

"Aunt Rachel, I couldn't sleep under this quilt," I answered softly, putting my hand over hers. "Wouldn't be restful, somehow. Anyway, I think it should stay here. Maybe others can use it."

Aunt Rachel sighed. "But aine you gon' need the quilt where you goin'?"

I kissed her. "Don't worry, Aunt Rachel. I got the memory of it in my head."

It rained hard for three days the next week. Me and Jack left Home Plantation in a dark thunderstorm. The day after, it was too stormy to work in the fields, so Jack wasn't missed. And Aunt Rachel told them I was sick.

We went north, following the trail of the freedom quilt. All the things people told me about, all the tiny stitches I took, now I could see real things. There was the old tree struck down by lightning, the winding road near the creek, the hunting path through the swamp. It was like being in a dream you already dreamed.

Mostly we hid during the day and walked at night. When we got to North Farm, Jack slipped in through the darkness to find what cabin my momma at. Then we went in to get her and found a little sister I didn't even know I had. Momma was so surprised.

"Sweet Clara! You growed so big!" Her eyes just like I remembered, her arms strong around me.

"Momma, I'm here for you. We goin' North. We know the way."

I was afraid they wouldn't come. But then Momma say
yes. Young Jack carried my sister Anna, and I held on to
Momma's hand.

We kept on as fast as we could, skirting farms and
towns and making our way through the woods. At last, one
clear dark night, we come to the Ohio River. The river was
high, but I remembered the place on the quilt where I'd
marked the crossing. We searched the brush along the
banks until at last we found the little boat.

"This was hid here by the folks in the Underground
Railroad," I said.

The boat carried us across the dark, deep water to the
other side. Shivering and hungry and scared, we stood
looking ahead.

"Which way now?" Jack asked me.

I pointed. The North Star was shining clear above us. "Up there through the woods. North. To Canada."

Sometimes I think back to the night we left, when Young Jack come to wake me. I can still see Aunt Rachel sitting up in her bed. She just shook her head before I could say a word.

"Before you go, just cover me with your quilt, Sweet Clara," she say. "I'm too old to walk, but not too old to dream. And maybe I can help others follow the quilt to freedom."

Aunt Rachel kept her word. The quilt is there still, at Home Plantation. People go look at it, even folks from neighbouring farms. I know because some of them come

and tell me how they used it to get free. But not all are as lucky as we were, and most never can come.

Sometimes I wish I could sew a quilt that would spread over the whole land, and the people just follow the stitches to freedom, as easy as taking a Sunday walk.

AFTER YOU READ

Make a character portrait

To make a character portrait, you tell about someone by using words instead of pictures. Write a character portrait of Clara. Tell who she is and where she lives. Tell about her personality. You will find out about her personality by looking at what she says, thinks, and does, and what other people in the story say about her.

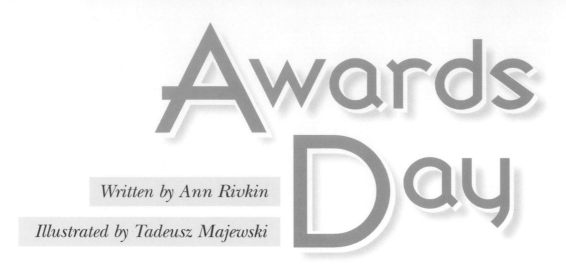

Awards Day

Written by Ann Rivkin

Illustrated by Tadeusz Majewski

From his bedroom window, eleven-year-old Steve Nesrallah could see the boat "West Wind" tied up at the dock. He knew that all around the bay the other kids would soon be down at their family floats, waiting for his father to pick them up and take them to meet the school bus.

Most mornings he was at the dock, ready and waiting before it was time to leave. But not today. Today was the end of term, the day when Certificates of Merit were given out.

If Steve hadn't broken his arm last month everything would have been all right. He would have been getting two awards for sure—one for sports and one for perfect attendance. Now he would get nothing. He wouldn't have minded so much if it had not been that all the other kids on "West Wind" would be getting something. Especially David Hardy.

46

"David'll be the worst," Steve thought. "He's got six certificates coming to him at least and he's such a bragger. He'll be waving his bits of paper under my nose for all he's worth. If only ... if only something would go wrong today so 'West Wind' wouldn't start."

Steve clapped his hand over his mouth, hardly able to believe he had thought such a thing. He loved "West Wind" and he loved his job as his father's assistant. He kept the windows clear of flying spray, made sure everyone wore lifebelts, and looked out for the deadheads and drifting logs that were an ever-present danger on the B.C. coast.

A moment later he was startled by a sudden bang from below and his mother's voice calling up to him, loud and urgent. "Steve! Steve, come quick!"

He raced downstairs to see his father lying on the porch, one foot twisted back awkwardly under him.

"What happened?" he asked.

"Dad slipped," his mother said. "Be careful—it's like glass out here. It froze last night and we've had so much rain."

As she took one of her husband's arms, Steve took the other. Despite Mr. Nesrallah's protests that he could manage, they helped him into the living room and onto the couch. When he was settled, Mrs. Nesrallah made an ice-pack while Steve ran to the radio telephone to put in a call for a doctor.

"How is he?" Steve asked, as his mother came into the kitchen.

"It's his ankle. It's swelling badly. It might even be broken. Mainly though he's worrying about the kids missing school, especially with Awards Day and the end-of-term party."

A queer guilty feeling gripped at Steve as he remembered his wish of earlier that morning.

"It's no one's fault," he blurted out.

"Of course not," his mother replied reassuringly. "But you know how Dad is. Things like this matter to him. His people have always been seafarers. He keeps saying over and over that when he promises his boat will do a job that job must be done."

Steve smiled, feeling he could almost hear words rolling off his father's tongue. "If I say 'West Wind' will pick up kids, they will be picked up." With that, an idea came to him. His smile died and he bent his head, shuffling his feet.

He could take "West Wind," couldn't he? He'd handled her in all kinds of weather and he knew every inch of the way but.... But there was still David Hardy and his armful of awards.

All at once Steve found himself pulling on his jacket, taking up his lunch pail, and walking to the door.

"I'll pick the kids up," he said.

"Are you sure?" his mother sounded concerned. "It's a big responsibility."

He gave her a quick grin. "I'm part seafarer too, remember," he answered, running for the dock before he could change his mind.

The day was sunny with no wind. Skimming through the shining water, Steve began to feel his worries disappear.

He was skipper now, a captain for a day. Let David Hardy have his certificates. He, Steve, was in charge. He turned the wheel with a flourish as he reached the Hardy float.

"Where's your dad, today?" David asked.

"He had an accident. I'm taking over."

"You're going to do everything, all by yourself?"

Steve opened his mouth to say, "Sure," but right away he realized that, try as he might, he couldn't attend to the navigating and at the same time keep an eye on his passengers. He swallowed hard.

"Will you take charge of the younger kids for me, Dave?" he asked.

He was more than glad of David's help when they reached the Reed family float.

"Hey look, Mr. Nesrallah isn't here today," Pat Reed called out, leaping into "West Wind" and making her rock about wildly.

"Great," Johnny Reed added, tossing his lifebelt to one side. "I'm not wearing this."

"Oh yes you are," David said, grabbing each of them in turn and adjusting their lifebelts. "Now sit down and keep still," he ordered, "or I'll throw you into the saltchuck with the fish."

The journey continued. Now that the Reeds were settled there shouldn't be any problems, Steve thought. Soon he would see little Sue Jones standing at the water's edge waving, then the Becker twins, then the bus terminal. But he didn't see Sue. In fact, suddenly, he couldn't see anything at all. There was a horrible feeling inside him as he strained his eyes through the thick mist that had come up to surround them totally. He remembered his father's warning about bright days in winter, wishing he had listened more carefully.

"Warm sun on cold water, sometimes that brings fog," Mr. Nesrallah had said many times.

With the familiar landmarks all blotted out, there was nothing to steer by but the compass. Steve checked the small instrument and found he was on the right course. Still it seemed like forever before he heard a muffled "Hello-o" and a float with two ghostly figures on it appeared.

David reached over and lifted the small figure on board. "Hi, Sue," he said.

"Awful thick, isn't it, Mr. Nesrallah, but I know you can make it," Mrs. Jones, the taller figure, called out.

Steve mumbled a reply. It wasn't till after they had pulled away from the dock that it occurred to him that Mrs. Jones had thought his father was at the wheel. Probably, she wouldn't have let Sue go otherwise. He knew then what his mother had meant about a big responsibility.

There was no time for worrying though. Now he had to find a way to reassure the younger ones. Already Pat was asking in a frightened voice, "How will the other boats see us in all this?"

Desperate, Steve let his mind go back to a story his father had told, of a time when Mr. Nesrallah was still in Lebanon before he came to Canada, when he was working as a fisherman out of his small village and a boat he was on was wrecked.

"We'll sing songs and let them hear us. How's that?" Steve said.

Sue and the Reeds looked doubtful but again David came to Steve's aid. "Good idea. Let's start," he agreed and he began to sing in a loud voice until the others joined in.

"Thanks, Dave," Steve muttered, staring once more into the swirling mist.

Was that two dim lights he could see ahead? They shone palely, moving from side to side. Were they on land or on water? He wasn't sure but they did seem to be in the direction he had to go. He moved on, letting out a cheer

when his eyes picked out the Becker twins swinging flashlights to and fro.

"You're a couple of smart kids," he told them gratefully.

He now had all his passengers on board. He knew that they were entering a narrow pass and would soon reach a huge cliff with jagged edges that could rip "West Wind" in two. The others knew it as well. They had stopped singing and were sitting very still.

Steve drew a deep breath. Again he thought of his father. "You know what we're going to do?" he said. "We're going to sound for echoes so we'll know where the cliff is. Everyone'll have to help. David will blow the whistle and we'll count the number of seconds it takes the sound to reach the cliff and come back. The echo moves at five seconds to a mile, so we'll be able to figure where we are. Okay?"

"Okay," everyone chorused.

David gave a loud blast on the whistle.

"One...."

The echo bounced back immediately and with a gasp Steve threw the engine into reverse, hurriedly swinging the wheel at the same time.

The sound had come from dead ahead. The jagged cliff was only a few hundred feet away and they had been heading directly toward it. In another minute....

Steve's voice was breathless as he said, "Let's see how far away we are now."

David blew the whistle again, and again they began to count. This time the echo was well to starboard. If they kept in a straight line without veering at all, they ought to be in the clear.

Steve's hands gripped the wheel tightly. Slowly, carefully, he inched his way, now in neutral, now "ahead." The fog still covered everything.

"I think we should test again," he said.

David blew another blast.

"One, two...."

The echo bounced from beyond the stern. The cliff was behind them. They were safe.

"Whew!" Steve wiped his forehead, then blinked and held his hand up high. Was that a breeze he felt on his fingers? His father had a saying for that too.

"Wind or fog, one or the other. But never the two together. Not ever!"

They were coming out of the narrow pass now and into open water. A puff of wind touched Steve's face. Trails of vapour began to drift upward and the mist thinned slowly into a cloudy sky.

It was several minutes before he could see really clearly but, at last, they rounded the point and the terminal came into view.

There was the orange and black school bus, and the dock with the four other school launches. On the wharf a crowd had gathered, waving to them and cheering.

"Oh boy, look at that," Steve said, as he eased "West Wind" toward the dock.

People crowded around him then, shaking his hand and offering congratulations. He was told not to worry about the homeward journey. The fog would be gone for the day. Even better he was given a message from home. The doctor had been and there were no bones broken in his father's leg.

"Your father was on the radio telephone himself," Mr. Jackson, the school bus driver said.

"He had a special word he wanted me to tell you but I couldn't get it. He said it meant 'son of a seafarer' in his own language. There was something else too, about some ancient guys—the Phoenicians?"

Steve grinned to show he understood and looked 'round for David. In all the turmoil they had become separated and yet he felt that David should be sharing this moment of triumph. To his disappointment he saw that "West Wind's" passengers had gone off on their own. They were huddled together whispering and they obviously didn't want anyone else to hear. With his head bent, feeling left out, he started toward the school bus.

Suddenly, there was a patter of feet behind him. He turned to see Sue Jones. She thrust something into his hand, something rolled up and tied with string.

Wonderingly, he opened it. He found a sheet of lined paper torn from a school exercise book.

"CERTIFICATE OF MERIT," it said in capitals. "To Steve Nesrallah, from his friends."

He read it three times, knowing that though the printing was Sue's best Grade 1 style the words must have been spelled by David.

Happiness bubbled inside him. Next thing he knew he was surrounded by a ring of smiling faces.

"Do you like it?" Sue asked, eagerly.

Holding the certificate tightly, Steve looked from one to the other. He knew that, for him, this was the award that really counted.

"Thanks, all of you," he said. "You've made this into the best Awards Day I've ever had."

AFTER YOU READ

Identify cause and effect

Make a chart like the one below. In the first column, record each event in the story that caused something else to happen. In the second column, record the decision the characters made to respond to this event. In the last column, record the effect of this decision.

Cause	Decision Made	Effect
- Mr. Nesrallah falls and can't drive the boat	- Steve will drive the boat	- students can go to school

WORKING TOGETHER
with
ONE HEART

. . . .

READING TIP

Use picture clues

Photographs can provide you with information to help you understand what you are reading. Look carefully at the photographs before you read the text. What do they tell you about Canadians working together?

There are times when working alone is totally satisfying. You concentrate all your efforts on what you are doing and feel proud of the results. Working together with others has a different feel. You realize how much in common you have with others and accomplish results that no one could bring about alone. The following articles show two different ways in which Canadians have found to work together to develop and share their talents.

LEARNING GOALS

You will

• read about two examples of Canadians working together

• use photographs to find information

56

The Arctic Winter Games

Written by Todd Mercer

The Arctic Winter Games bring people together from a wide northern area to compete in athletic events and share their unique cultures.

Participants come from the Yukon, the Northwest Territories, and northern Alberta in Canada; Alaska in the United States; and Greenland and Russia.

There is a rich mix of northern cultures. For example, at Games' events you might hear such languages as Inupiaq, Yupik, Aleut, Slavey, Gwich'in, Chipewyan, Tlingit, Tsimshian, Inuktitut, Inuvlaluktun, French, and English.

The Games came about when a few people noticed that northern athletes were sometimes unable to successfully compete against fellow athletes from the South. Athletes from the North often lacked athletic facilities and had fewer athletes to compete against or join their teams.

The first Arctic Winter Games were in Yellowknife in 1970, when 500 athletes participated. Today well over 1600

57

athletes, coaches, organizers, and cultural performers take part. The Games happen every two years. There are usually around 20 different sports, and events range from figure skating and indoor soccer to cross-country skiing, dog sledding, and snow shoeing.

Traditional Arctic sports are among the most popular events. These include Inuit and Dene Games.

Competition is strong as athletes try to win awards presented to the top three competitors in each event. Medals are gold, silver, and bronze, and are shaped like Ulus (traditional Inuit scraping knives).

Winning is just one of the athletic goals celebrated at the Arctic Winter Games. The Hodgson trophy is awarded to the regional team whose athletes best display the ideals of fair play. As well, Fair Play Pins are awarded to participants who strive toward fair play and friendly competition.

The logo communicates the values of the Arctic Winter Games. The three interlocking rings stand for the Games' three major goals: "to encourage maximum participation of all ages and cultures in athletic competition and to foster cultural exhibitions and social interchange." The strong northern character of the Games is seen in the logo picture of the aurora borealis, or northern band of lights.

ARCTIC
WINTER
GAMES

Then again, maybe the Games' true spirit is best captured by Julia Oolayou, a competitor from Baffin Island. She says the Arctic Winter Games are "a good way of meeting new friends and keeping our culture alive."

58

Jesse Ketchum Pan Vibrations

Written by Todd Mercer

Pan Vibrations is the talented steel band of Jesse Ketchum school in Toronto, Ontario. The band program began in 1994 and now includes 90 students from grades 3 to 8 in a school of just under 600 pupils.

Pan music was born in Trinidad many years ago. Since some people couldn't afford expensive instruments, they created their own out of found materials, such as garbage cans and industrial containers. The unique music made from these homemade instruments, called *pans,* is a great source of Caribbean pride. In 1992, pans became the national instrument of Trinidad and Tobago.

The idea for a Canadian school steel band started when Jesse Ketchum teacher Heather McIvor visited Tobago. She saw a large student steel band and thought it would be a great idea for her school. When she returned to Toronto, she phoned Cecil Clarke at the Pan Trinbago Association in Toronto, the major organization for steel bands in Canada. Cecil agreed to help.

and performed at concerts in Sudbury, Peterborough, and Montreal. In 1996, the band went on a three-week tour of Trinidad and Tobago, making them the first Canadian elementary school steel band to tour outside the country.

Pan Vibrations is a shining example of cooperation. Band leader Cecil Clarke says that by playing in a large band, the students "are learning to communicate with one another. It takes teamwork."

Adds Heather McIvor, playing in the band "teaches students acceptance. They are working together when they're performing. Everybody is doing the same thing. It's all for one."

Student interest and hard work guarantee the program's continued success. Fundraising activities pay for instruments, uniforms, and trips.

The band obtains strong support from the local downtown community. Sometimes local businesses hire the band to perform at promotional events.

Often, the students use their musical talents to help

Heather and Cecil introduced a single steel pan into a school concert. The unique instrument fascinated almost every student. Within months, a student steel band program was in place.

Their song list includes a wide range of musical styles, from popular to jazz, calypso, reggae, rhythm and blues, rock and roll, and classical.

Band members practise all year. And the hard work pays off with continually improving musical skills. They've won many youth steel band competitions causes they strongly believe in. For example, the band has performed to raise money for the preservation of a local water shed and has entertained at a camp for children suffering from sickle cell anemia and at the Special Olympics.

Heather McIvor sums it up when she says, "We want to give back to the community, because people have been good to us."

Besides steel pans, band musicians also play such percussion instruments as timbales, tumbas, congas, shakers, and regular drums.

AFTER YOU READ

Give your opinion

Why do you think this selection is called "Working Together with One Heart"? Use information from the text and the photographs to give evidence for your answer.

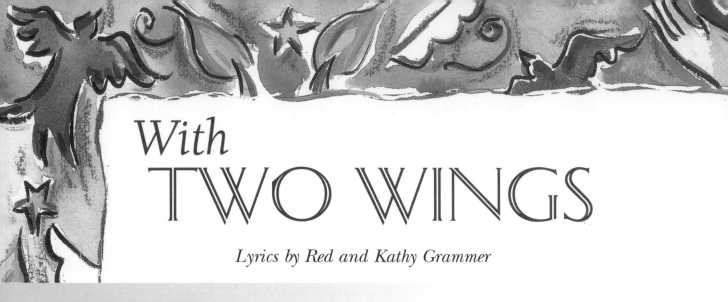

With
TWO WINGS

Lyrics by Red and Kathy Grammer

READING TIP

Set a purpose for reading

Think about some times when you needed someone to help you. Brainstorm a list of words that describe how you feel when someone helps you. How do you feel when you help someone else? As you read the lyrics for this song, find out the message the author is giving you about working together.

Chorus

All:
With two wings
We can soar through the air
With two wings
We can go most anywhere
With two wings
We can sail through the sky
With two wings
We can fly.

All:
Repeat Chorus

Voice 1:
I am one wing father and brother
By myself all I can do is flutter
I'm only one wing
I need the other
For the dove of peace to fly.

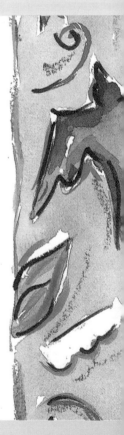

Voice 2:   I am one wing sister and mother
By myself all I can do is flutter
I'm only one wing
I need the other
For the dove of peace to fly.

All: Repeat Chorus

Voice 1:   I am one voice.
Voice 2:   I am another.
Voice 1:   I'm half the world.
Voice 2:   I am the other.
All: When we learn to work together
Then the dove of peace will fly.

All: Repeat Chorus

AFTER YOU READ

Use examples in your response

Why do you think this song is called "With Two Wings"? Use examples from the song and your own life to support your answer.

Making a Difference

In this unit, you have read about people and story characters who made a difference in their world. Now it is your turn to write an oral report and make a short presentation about how you, too, can make a difference—in your family, your school, or your community.

▶ Before You Begin

Choose an idea from one of the selections in this unit as the focus for your report or think of your own way to make a difference. Ask yourself these questions:

- What can I do that will make a difference?
- Who or what will my actions help?
- How will I know if I made a difference?
- Who will hear and see my presentation?
- How can I make my presentation interesting for my audience?

> ### Ideas
>
> ▶ Clean up the environment.
> ▶ Do extra chores at home.
> ▶ Help someone who is sick.
> ▶ Spend time with someone who is lonely.

Here is an example of how Todd planned to make a difference. He created a chart on his computer to organize his thoughts.

Action Plan: Make my grandmother happy	
Why	**How**
- she loves to play the piano at the nursing home	- I'll play piano at the nursing home
- she has arthritis and can't play the piano anymore	- I'll ask people at the nursing home if it would be all right to play
- other people might enjoy music too	

▶ Your First Draft

Write a report about what you are going to do to make a difference. Your written draft will help you to prepare for your oral presentation.

1 **Write an Introduction**
- The first paragraph should tell what your report is about. It should tell what you have chosen to do to make a difference. It should also say something to "hook" your audience.

Here is how Todd started his written report.

> Toes tapping, hands clapping, swaying in their chairs. Wrinkled smiles, glistening eyes, memories of yesterday. Lots of nods and loud applause. Playing piano at my grandma's nursing home makes everyone involved feel good.

2 **Write the Middle, or *Body,* of the Report**
- This is the main part of your report. Tell why you think your action is important and how you went about achieving your action plan.
- Use "order" words to explain to your audience the steps you followed in your action plan.

first   next   last

Todd then wrote about his action plan.

> My parents told me I need to practise the piano more, so I decided to play for Grandma. First, I asked my parents if I could practise at the nursing home.

3 **Write a Conclusion**
- The end of your report should tell how you feel about what you have done to make a difference.

Here is how Todd ended his report.

> People who live in nursing homes need to enjoy life and music, too! Watching and hearing their responses made me feel great, like I've really made a difference.

▶ Prepare an Oral Report

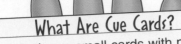

1 Make Cue Cards

- Write each of the main ideas from your report on a cue card.
- Under the main idea, write down a few points to help you remember what else you want to say.
- Include a cue card to help you remember your opening and your conclusion.

Remember to number the cards to help you keep them in order.

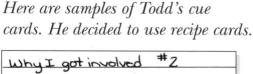

What Are Cue Cards?

Cue cards are small cards with notes to guide you during your presentation. You can hold cue cards in the palm of your hand. When you are speaking to an audience, you can use them to help you remember your ideas.

Here are samples of Todd's cue cards. He decided to use recipe cards.

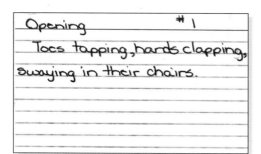

Opening   # 1
   Toes tapping, hands clapping, swaying in their chairs.

Why I got involved   # 2
- grandma can't play
- has arthritis

2 Practise Your Presentation

- Read your written report over many times so you really know it.
- Practise your presentation using your cue cards to help you.
- Look at each card, then practise talking about your ideas.
- Practise in front of an audience.
- Start to practise several days before you give your talk: it takes time to get ready for an oral presentation.

Be your own audience!

Why not tape your presentation and listen to it as if you were sitting in the audience?

▶ Put It All Together

Here are some ways you might make your presentation more interesting.

- Bring pictures or slides to show while you present your report.
- Use your hands while you speak and use an expressive voice to emphasize the parts of your report you feel strongly about.
- Make eye contact with your audience to make them feel involved and keep their interest.

Try This If your action plan helped some people, they might be interested in hearing your report. Why not share it with them, too?

 ## Revise and Edit

Go back and review your presentation.

- Does your presentation flow smoothly?
- Do your cue cards help you to remember what you wanted to say?
- Is your presentation the right length?
- Will your presentation keep the interest of your audience? Should you add anything or leave anything out?
- Does your vocabulary keep your audience interested?
- Is your grammar correct?
- Do you need to speak more slowly, loudly, or clearly?

 ## Think about Your Learning

Add other ideas to help you the next time you write a report and present it to the class.

- Did you choose an issue that was important to you?
- Did you get permission to act on your plan?
- Did you think about who or what you would help by your actions?
- Was your action plan described step-by-step?
- Did you think of a good introduction and conclusion for your oral report?
- Did you make cue cards to help you remember your ideas?
- Did you take enough time to practise your presentation?

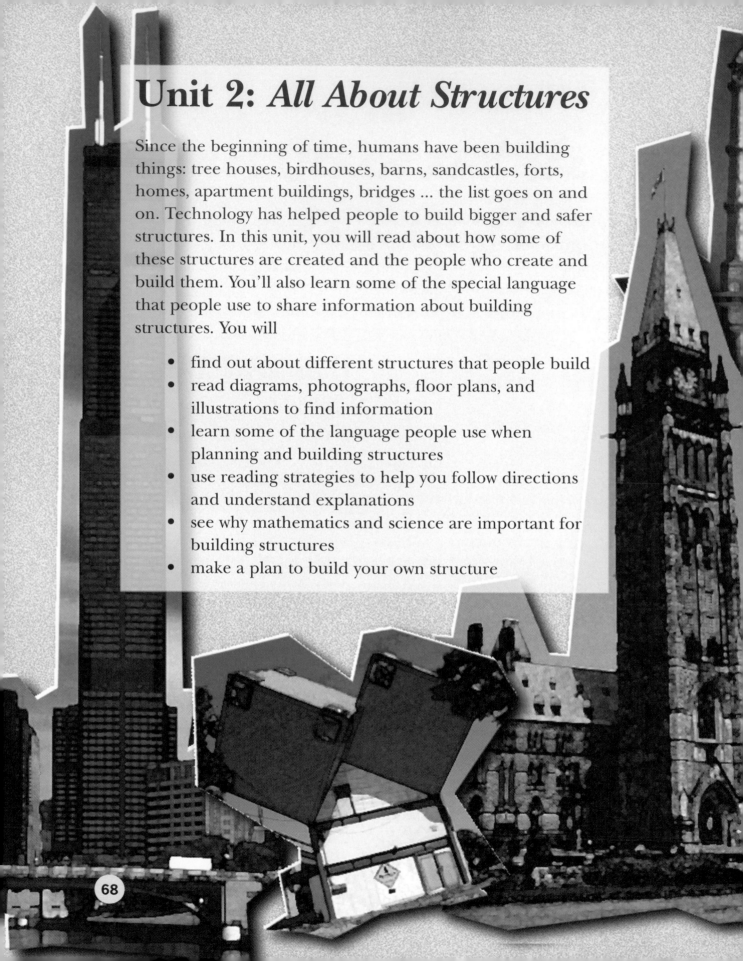

Unit 2: *All About Structures*

Since the beginning of time, humans have been building things: tree houses, birdhouses, barns, sandcastles, forts, homes, apartment buildings, bridges ... the list goes on and on. Technology has helped people to build bigger and safer structures. In this unit, you will read about how some of these structures are created and the people who create and build them. You'll also learn some of the special language that people use to share information about building structures. You will

- find out about different structures that people build
- read diagrams, photographs, floor plans, and illustrations to find information
- learn some of the language people use when planning and building structures
- use reading strategies to help you follow directions and understand explanations
- see why mathematics and science are important for building structures
- make a plan to build your own structure

Natural Builders

Adapted by Susan Green

READING TIP

Read photographs

A photo essay gives information through pictures and captions. Look carefully at the photographs before reading the captions. What do all the photographs have in common?

Everyone is a builder at some time in their lives. When you were younger, you probably built sandcastles or liked to stack blocks. Maybe you built tree houses or snow forts. All it took was a little bit of imagination.

Today, you might think building such things are just kid stuff. There are many adults, however, who would disagree with you. Here are some adult creations that might remind you of the things you built when you were young.

These adults play with Lego bricks all day long. They use thousands of Lego bricks at a time to build dinosaurs, people, spaceships, and many other fantastic creations. They are architects and scientists, but building with Lego is what they most like to do. Each creation takes from a day to several weeks to make. The master builders have been described as "making poetry out of plastic." Their models are sent all over the world and put on display so that people can see what kinds of things can be built with these tiny multicoloured interlocking bricks.

Pictured here are some master Lego builders and their creations.

These pictures of tree houses appeared in *Smithsonian* magazine.

If you have ever played in a tree house, you know it is a wonderful place to escape—from a pesky brother or sister, to read a book, or just to take some time and think. There are many adults who feel the same way and are still building tree houses—only now they build the houses as places in which to live.

Maple, oak, and hemlock trees are used most often by tree house architects. The branches on which the platform for a house rests must be at least 15 cm in diameter. Architects built the tree houses shown here without harming the trees. Many builders even use straps instead of nails to fix a house in place.

These sandcastles are very different in size and style.

Wherever there's sand, there is bound to be someone making sandcastles. Some adults have turned a childhood interest in building with sand into a lifelong hobby. Sandcastle builders travel the world to participate in competitions and exhibit the castles, creatures, and communities they can make out of sand and water. The sculptures are sometimes more than six storeys tall and use as much as 3060 m^3 of sand. Some of these amazing sandcastles are put on permanent display in malls and other public areas, while others are left at the beach to wash away with the tide.

AFTER YOU READ

Compare information

What gave you the most information about these builders: the photographs or the words? Do you think a photo essay is a good way to communicate information? Tell your reasons why or why not.

MEET THE Architects

Written by Todd Mercer

READING TIP

Read interview questions

In an interview, the questions are just as important as the answers. Make a list of questions you would ask if you were going to interview an architect. Skim through the selection and read all of the questions before you read the answers.

How do architects design buildings? What role do they play while the building is under construction? I asked Canadian architects Kim Storey and Douglas Cardinal those questions, and more.

LEARNING GOALS

You will

- read about the careers of three Canadian architects

- learn what makes a good interview question

Kim Storey

Kim Storey's architecture has won international attention. One of Kim's recent projects shows how she designs buildings and the open spaces around them.

When did you decide you wanted to become an architect?

My father was an architect in Chatham, Ontario. So I grew up with architecture all around me. At a very young age, I went to his office and saw what architects do. I helped him by delivering architectural drawings. From those early experiences, I knew I wanted to be an architect.

What interests did you have as a child that have helped you in your work as an architect?

I've always loved art. Also, reading has been a tremendous help to my career. People sometimes think architects just solve the technical problems of building. That's important, but a major part of my work is creating designs. You need ideas to create. I find many ideas through reading.

What does an architect do?

Clients often have different ideas about what they want in a new building. One person might want fresh air and many open windows. Another might want the building to be air-conditioned. A good architect considers all these requests and creates a building proposal that serves clients' needs and works for the surrounding community.

How do you develop your ideas?

My husband and I are partners. We often draw and re-draw sketches to develop ideas. Even at home we spend time drawing, thinking, and talking about projects. Discussion is very important. If you keep ideas to yourself, they might not be as good as you first think. You have to test your ideas by sharing them with others.

What was the role of the architect in building the Coronation Park Pavilion?

We created models showing three different ways of solving the design problems and presented them to our clients. Fortunately, the clients chose the idea we liked best.

The Coronation Park Pavilion in Toronto had many interesting design problems. The building needed change rooms for swimmers, locker rooms for baseball teams, and washrooms for people using the nearby cycling trail. It also required Park offices on the second floor.

Then we developed design drawings and a more detailed model. We showed these to the clients and asked for their comments. They made suggestions such as, "We want this room bigger" or "We need more office space."

Floor plans for the Coronation Park Pavilion. The legend will help you to read these plans.

Legend			
1	covered walkway	6	team change room
2	future concession stand	7	park storage
3	phone	8	bridge
4	fountain	9	staff area
5	public washroom	10	lunchroom
		11	office

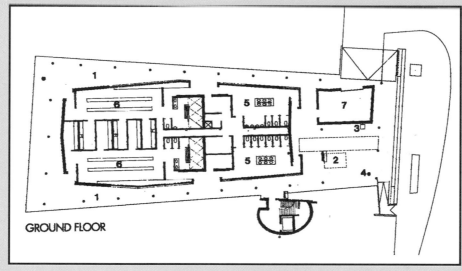

GROUND FLOOR

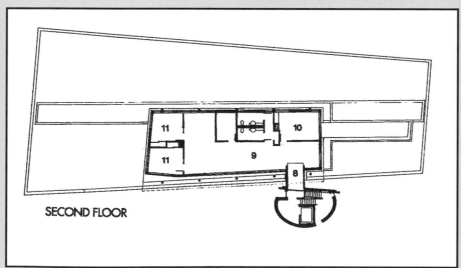

SECOND FLOOR

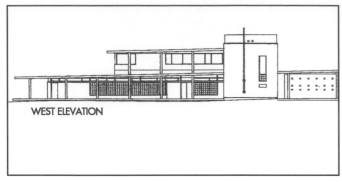

WEST ELEVATION

An *elevation* like the one here shows what a building looks like from the outside.

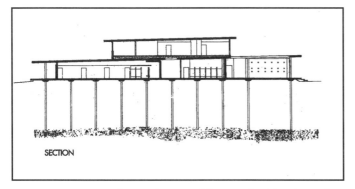

SECTION

A *section* provides an inside view of a building as if it were sliced open.

At the same time, we were developing floor plans and drawings of how the building would work. We created a series of views, called *elevations* and *sections*, showing the building as you moved around it.

Then we reached a point where the clients had a clear picture of our ideas and said, "This is the building we'd like you to build." Architects call this approval step *sign-off*.

Then we worked on the highly detailed working drawings. This required us to create drawings showing every building face and surface.

A model of the Coronation Park Pavilion.

We produced a thick document called the *specifications*. This book gives details of all materials and instructions for building.

Contractors who want to construct the various building systems then bid for the work. You might have people bidding to do the building construction, the electrical system, or the plumbing. Usually, the person with the lowest bid wins the work.

The next stage is the construction stage. The contractor takes our drawings and starts to build. As architects, we have to make sure the contractors are building exactly as we've instructed.

What advice would you give to kids who want to become architects?

You have to understand that architecture is not just about nuts and bolts. It's also about ideas. The profession requires lots of training—sometimes up to eleven years.

However, the good side is you can spend your whole life doing it. Architecture is not something you're going to get bored with. Every job we've had is entirely different from the last. That's really exciting.

Douglas Cardinal

Douglas Cardinal is also a well-known Canadian architect. One of his most famous buildings is the Museum of Civilization in Hull, Quebec.

Douglas was born in Calgary and raised on a farm outside Red Deer. His father was a game warden whose deep love of nature was a part of his Blackfoot heritage. Douglas has also passed on this love of the land through the buildings he creates. Their curving shapes resemble landscape forms.

What were some of the things you had to consider in designing the Museum?

Once I had my idea of the design for the museum's inside, I placed it on the site using my computer. The computer gave me the freedom to make changes where required and to experiment with my ideas. I tried flattening the shape of the building to see how that worked. I had to be concerned about the winds around Ottawa, so I twisted and moulded the form to take these winds into account.

I had to be very concerned not to spoil the view around our capital. I didn't want the museum to hide people's view of Canada's Parliament Buildings. My computer allowed me to pull and shift the museum so that it didn't hide the other buildings.

How do you work?

Everything I design is drawn on the computer. There are no drawing boards in the office. The computer creates a picture of the whole building for us. It automatically gives us the size of the building and the areas within it. The Museum of Civilization has many curves. It's much harder to get an idea of the size of a curved building than it is for a square building. A computer can give you the size in seconds.

What gives you the most satisfaction about being an architect?

Architecture, when it's done well, is an art. It's probably the art that has the most effect on people's lives— because they use or see buildings every day.

And it's nice to know you've made a lasting contribution.

Frank
Gehry

Frank Gehry was born in Toronto and began building for fun as a child, using leftover scraps his grandmother had collected from a furniture maker. The Guggenheim Museum in Spain is one of many buildings he has designed through the years. It has recently brought him much acclaim.

The Guggenheim has a steel frame (weighing more than 4.5 million kilograms) that is covered with titanium. This coating catches the light of the sun and shimmers, making the building appear like a wriggling fish or a ship with sails billowing to some onlookers.

According to other architects, with the completion of the Guggenheim Museum, Frank has created "the greatest building of our time."

AFTER YOU READ

Write interview questions

Take a close look at Todd Mercer's interview questions. Pick out three of the questions you think obtained the best information from the architects. What do you think makes a good interview question? Look back at the interview questions and see if you can make them into better questions.

How to Build a House

Written by Trudee Romanek
Illustrated by Anne Stanley

READING TIP

Track sequence

Writers explain how something is made by telling readers what happens first, second, and so on. They will often give you clues to help you track the sequence of events by using "order" words such as "next," "then," "first," and "last." As you read, track the sequence of events involved in building a house. Use "order" words to help you.

There are a lot of different kinds of houses—houses made of bricks or wood, stones or logs, and having one floor, or two or three floors. No matter what the type of house, it usually takes many different experts to build one.

The first person involved is the architect, who makes many decisions about the house. What will it be made of? How many bedrooms will it have? Will there be a garage attached to it? The architect draws design sketches to show the final layout of the rooms in the house. Often, each floor, or *storey,* of the house has its own floor plan. The architect draws each floor plan as though we were looking down on the house from above.

Floor Plan

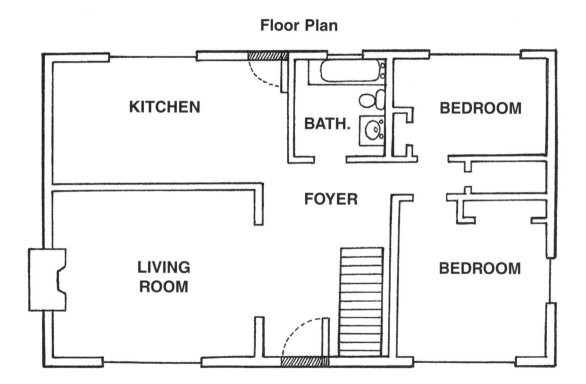

House Section

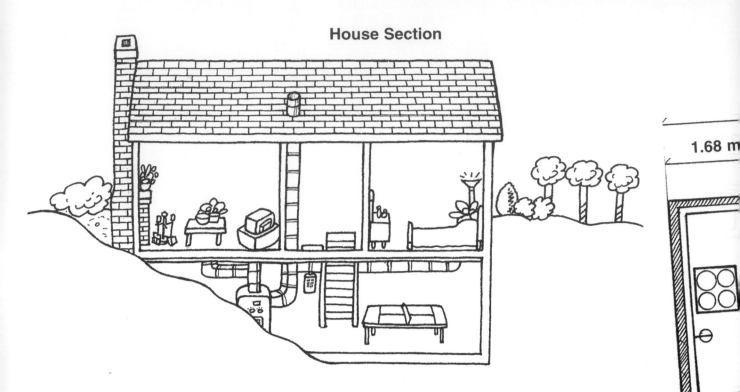

The architect also makes other drawings of what the finished house will look like, called *elevations* and *sections*. Each drawing shows the house from a different angle. This section shows the finished house from the front, as though the front wall has been removed.

Next, the architect makes working drawings. Copies of these detailed plans, called *blueprints*, will be used by the construction specialists as they build the house. Architects use special symbols to mark on the blueprints certain things that all houses have. Take a look at this legend to see what some of the symbols represent.

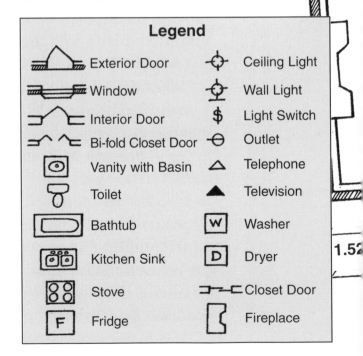

Legend	
Exterior Door	Ceiling Light
Window	Wall Light
Interior Door	Light Switch
Bi-fold Closet Door	Outlet
Vanity with Basin	Telephone
Toilet	Television
Bathtub	Washer
Kitchen Sink	Dryer
Stove	Closet Door
Fridge	Fireplace

Blueprint

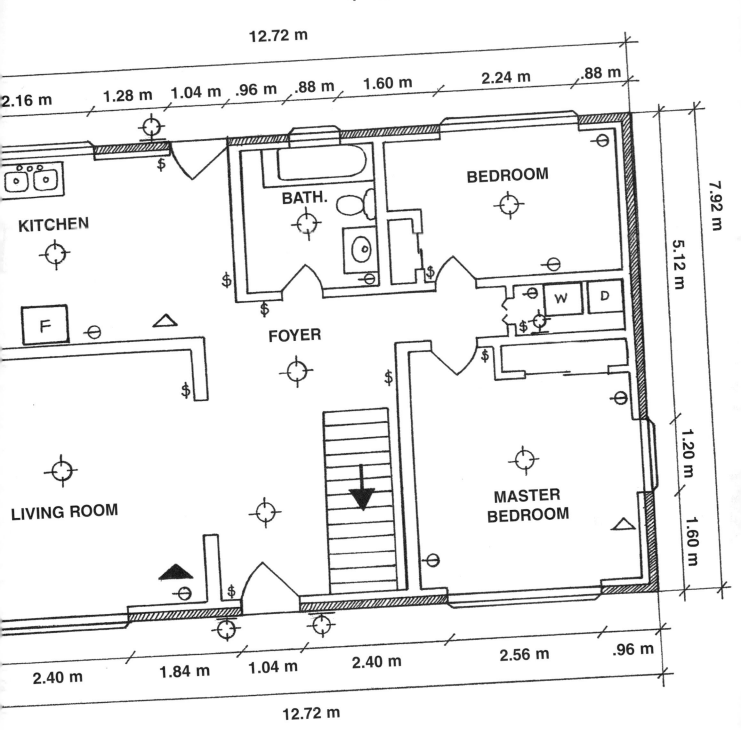

When the plans are final, the general contractor's job begins. It is his or her job to decide what supplies are needed, to hire a team of professionals to do the building work, and to keep everything on schedule.

Once the *site*—the piece of land where the house is to be built—has been chosen, the contractor hires a surveyor. The surveyor measures the site and uses stakes to mark the outline of where the house is to be built. Then the excavation team brings in heavy equipment to dig the hole for the house's foundation.

surveyor

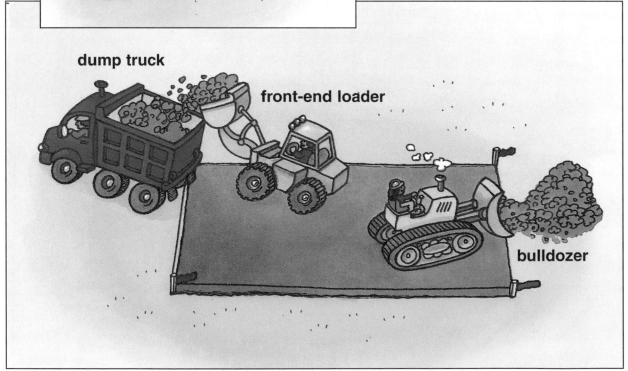

dump truck

front-end loader

bulldozer

In the bottom of the hole, foundation builders dig a trench where the walls will meet the ground. They line the trench with boards, and a cement mixer fills this form with concrete. This is called the *footing*.

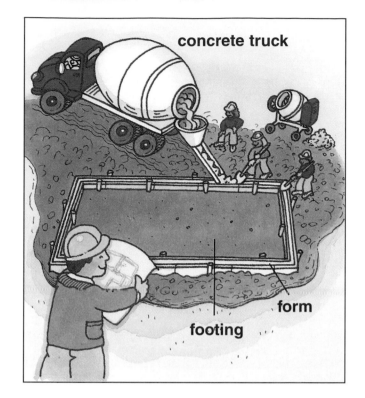

The foundation builders construct large wood forms on the hardened footing for the walls, and then pour concrete into them. Sometimes the walls of the foundation are built from concrete blocks, instead, which are stacked one on top of another, like bricks, with wet cement called *mortar* in between.

While these walls are hardening, the builders pour a layer of gravel into the bottom of the foundation hole. The cement mixer then pours concrete on top. The workers spread this concrete around to make a smooth floor.

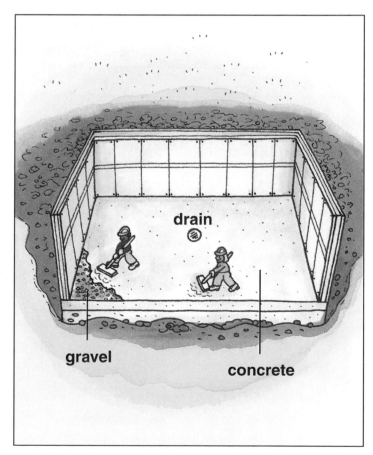

septic tank

tar

Once the walls have hardened, the workers remove the wood forms and coat the outside of the foundation with tar to keep water from seeping in. At the same time, the septic-system crew lays pipes from the house to the local water pipes. These pipes will bring clean water to the house. The septic-system crew also connects pipes from the house to the city sewer system or to a septic tank they have installed near the house. Those pipes will carry the used water away. If the house is to be heated by natural gas, the workers also put the gas lines in place.

The foundation of the house is now complete. The builders return some of the heavy equipment to the site to push dirt back in around the basement.

The carpentry crew now arrives at the site to build the wood frame for the house. First, they bolt boards on top of the foundation walls. This is called the *sill*. They next attach support beams, which rise up from the basement floor. On top of the sill and beams, they hammer wide boards, called *joists*, to make a frame. Then they nail plywood over the frame to make the floor, or *deck*, of the house. Once the deck is in place, the crew uses narrow boards to frame the walls, one at a time. They nail these boards into position.

The crew has framed all the inside and outside walls. Now

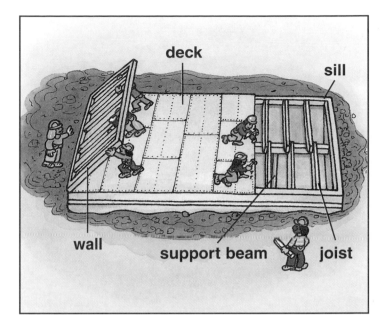

work on the roof can begin. The carpenters use medium-width boards, called *rafters*, to make the framework for the roof. On top of the rafters, they nail sheets of plywood.

The carpenters nail plywood sheets, or sometimes special Styrofoam sheets, to the outside of the exterior walls of the house. Then, they cover the roof and walls with tar paper or felt paper for protection against water. On the roof, the carpenters nail shingles over the protective paper, and the roof is complete.

A mason is hired to build a chimney for the house. The exterior doors and windows are added, too, to seal up the house against any bad weather that may come before it is completed.

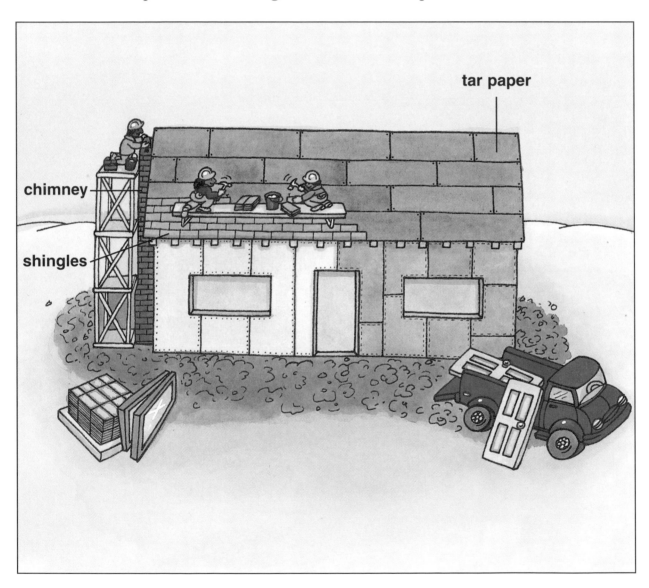

Inside, work crews begin to arrive. From now on, many people will be working in the house at once.

Electricians install a power box in the basement and run wires from the box to every room in the house. These wires will bring power to all of the outlets, lights, and switches.

Plumbers run pipes from the point where the water enters and leaves the foundation to each sink, toilet, and bathtub in the house.

A heating crew installs a furnace in the basement and ducts to take the warm air to every part of the house.

When all of these systems have been installed, an inspector checks the work to make sure everything is safe. Then the builders add the siding or brick outside walls of the house over the protective tar paper or felt paper.

water pipe

electrical wiring

furnace

power box

Insulation is placed between the studs of the framed walls and covered with a layer of plastic. Then a drywall crew nails drywall or gypsum board into place to form the inside walls. The crew spreads drywall compound thinly over the places where the pieces join to make the whole wall a smooth surface. Once the drywall is up, the carpenters add a frame around each window and door. Flooring crews install floors over the plywood decks.

All the final touches are put into the house. Painters cover the walls in a variety of colours. Plumbers install the bathroom fixtures and kitchen sinks. Cabinet makers or carpenters build the cupboards and put the counters in place. Electricians put in the light fixtures and switches. Appliances are installed in the kitchen and laundry room. Carpets are laid. Doors to the rooms are hung in the doorways. The inside of the house will soon be complete!

The landscaping crew arrives to finish the outside of the property. They smooth out the yard and plant trees, shrubs, and other plants. Then they seed the yard with grass or cover it with rolls of grass sod. The landscapers build walkways and pour the concrete front porch and steps.

All of the plumbers, electricians, carpenters, surveyors, and other specialists have prepared this house for the special moment when it becomes a home: the moment its new owners move in!

AFTER YOU READ

Make a flow chart

Make a flow chart like the one below. Use your chart to outline all of the steps involved in building a house.

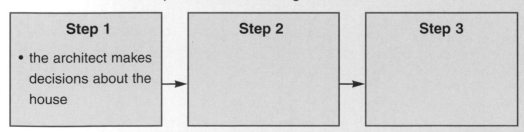

Step 1	Step 2	Step 3
• the architect makes decisions about the house		

Make a Model Room

Written by John Williams

READING TIP

Follow instructions

Writers give instructions by using action words that tell you exactly what to do. As you read, look for the action words in each step.

When a home has been designed and planned, it can then be built. Here are ideas for making a model room, with windows and doors.

A model like this is easy to glue if the glue is put on and then allowed to dry a little before pushing the pieces together.

You will need:

- stiff cardboard for base
- thick, soft cardboard for walls
- thin, see-through plastic for windows
- glue
- scraps of fabric
- pencil
- ruler
- scissors
- masking tape
- paint and paintbrush

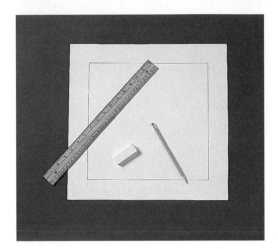

1 Find a piece of stiff cardboard. Using a pencil and ruler, mark the size and shape of the room you are going to make.

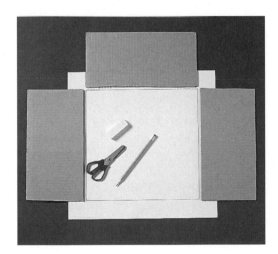

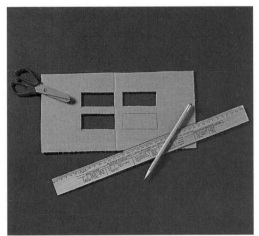

2 Measure the length of each wall on your plan and cut them out of thick cardboard. Each wall should be about 12 cm high.

3 Draw the shapes of the windows on the walls. Cut them out. Cut a piece of thin plastic to cover the window.

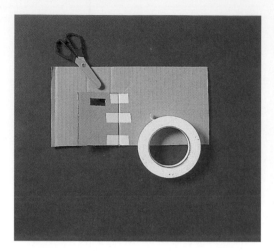

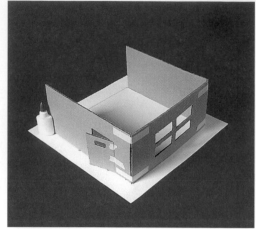

4 Cut a door shape in a wall. Make hinges out of masking tape and join the door to the wall down one side.

5 Attach the walls along the lines you drew in Step 1. Use small pieces of tape on the outside to hold the corners together if needed.

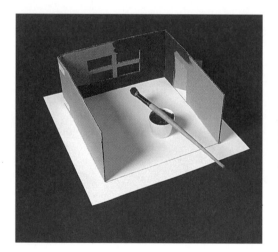

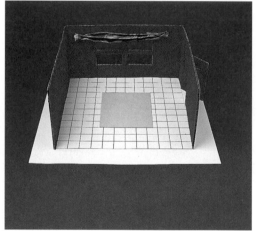

6 When the glue holding the walls together has dried, paint the insides of the walls, the window, and the door to look as real as possible.

7 You may wish to add scraps of fabric for curtains. You could also paint the floor to look like wood or cover it with felt to look like carpet.

Now Try This

If you enjoyed making this room, you could try making an entire home, with several different rooms. Or you could make a model of your own home.

Architects and builders often make models of buildings they are going to build. They make the models look as real as possible, with gardens, trees, cars, and even model people. This helps everyone see what the building will look like when it is finished.

AFTER YOU READ

Make a list

Make a list of the action words that helped you to follow the directions. How else did the writer make the instructions easy to follow?

The Little Pigs Housing Project

• • • • • •

Written by John McInnes
Illustrated by Steve Attoe

IN A SURPRISING TURN OF EVENTS, B. B. WOLF (FORMERLY KNOWN AS BIG BAD) HAS APOLOGIZED TO THE THREE LITTLE PIGS FOR DESTROYING AND DAMAGING THEIR HOMES. WOLF, NOW A DEVELOPER AND VEGETARIAN, HAS PROMISED TO HELP THEM REBUILD. THE PIGS ARE DELIGHTED AND WILL ASSIST WITH THE CONSTRUCTION. ON THE SIX O'CLOCK NEWS TONIGHT, ON CHANNEL 77, B. B. WOLF WILL PROVIDE MORE DETAILS IN A SPECIAL REPORT. THE THREE LITTLE PIGS WILL ALSO APPEAR.

Another great day in the village, Max.

Yes, and at the top of the news we have B. B. Wolf here to discuss his newsmaking project with homeowners The Three Little Pigs. Go ahead, B. B.

Thank you Max and Margot, and thank you Channel 77 for a chance to explain our building plans. Let me review a few principles of building houses.

Hound's
Hauling

Moose
transport

PIGLET CRES.

105

AFTER YOU READ

Identify fact and fiction

This story contains both factual information and fiction. Make a chart with three columns. In the first column, record what is factual information. In the second column, record what is fiction. In the last column, record anything about which you are not sure. How could you find out if it was fact or fiction?

Bridges

Written by Trudee Romanek
Illustrated by Bart Vallecoccia

READING TIP

Use headings to predict

Information writers often use special text features that fiction writers do not use. Sometimes they use headings as a way of organizing their information. Before you read this selection, scan the headings and predict what you think each section will be about.

If you've ever put a log or a board across a creek, you've made a bridge. There are many different types of bridges. Some are meant just for people to walk across, some are for cars, and others are for trains. Each one has a different way of holding up its own weight and the weight of the things that travel across it. Here are three of the main types of bridges.

Beam Bridge

A simple beam bridge is made of a single, strong crosspiece, called a *beam* or a *span,* with no supports underneath. This type of bridge is sometimes used to cross a low, narrow space. To cross a longer distance, several spans can be connected and supported from underneath by large posts, or *piers.*

Beam Bridge

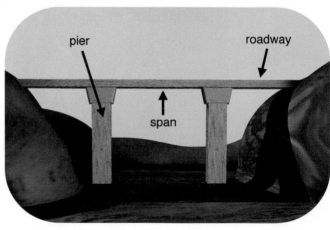

Arch Bridge

An arch bridge is made of curved pieces of steel. The pieces fit together to form an arch that reaches from one side of a space to the other. The crosspiece can rest on top of the arch, but it might also run through the middle or at the bottom of the arch. Straight pieces of steel, called *vertical struts*, connect the arch and the crosspiece. This kind of bridge is good for crossing areas that are too deep for piers—for example, river valleys.

Suspension Bridge

This kind of bridge is often built over water. It is made of two or more huge towers that are set into the lake or river bottom. Strong steel cables with huge concrete anchors at either end stretch between the towers. From these cables hang more wires, called *hangers*. The hangers attach to the roadway below and hold it up.

Arch Bridge

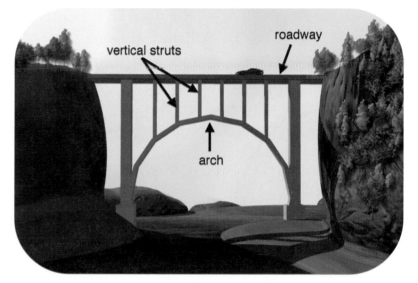

vertical struts roadway arch

Suspension Bridge

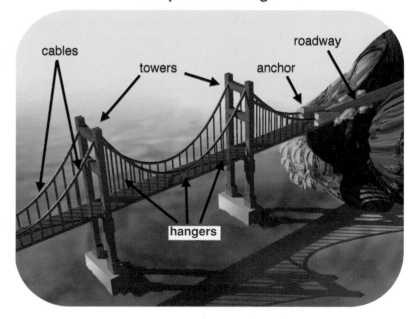

cables towers anchor roadway hangers

109

CONFEDERATION BRIDGE

Written by Trudee Romanek
Illustrated by Bart Vallecoccia and Tina Holdcroft

I n 1873, Prince Edward Island agreed to become a part of Canada. The islanders asked the government to provide continuous, year-round transportation from the island to the mainland. For 124 years, steamships, ice boats, and ice-breaking ferries carried passengers back and forth across the Northumberland Strait. All that has changed now.

On May 31, 1997, the Confederation Bridge opened. This 12.9-km bridge links Borden, P.E.I., with Jourimain Island, NB. It is one of the world's longest bridges and it was built in less than four years. For five months each winter, workers couldn't work in the strait because of ice. Many of the bridge pieces had to be made ahead of time on land

and then put in place once the ice cleared.

The Confederation Bridge is a beam bridge. It is made up of 44 spans. The largest span weighs 7500 t, about the same as 1500 elephants. A giant floating crane lowered each span into place. Information from as many as 10 satellites helped the crane position each span in just the right spot.

The engineers had to design a bridge that was extremely strong as well as long. Northumberland Strait is very windy and, in winter, is full of thick, heavy ice. Each winter and spring, chunks of ice up to 20 m thick travel south through the strait. Bridge designers were afraid that when a group of these huge chunks pushed against the bridge's piers, they might knock the piers over and collapse the bridge. The engineers had to come up with a way to break up the ice before it could do any damage. So, they tried a new shape for the piers.

Crossing the Bridge

Driving across the Confederation Bridge can take from 10 to 15 minutes at the usual speed limit of 80 km/h. If sensors on the bridge find that it's getting too windy, electronic signs on the bridge lower the speed limit.

Most bridge piers are cylinders, or columns. The Confederation Bridge piers are a little different. Each one has a cone-shaped ice shield around it that reaches from above the water level to below it. When an ice chunk comes to a pier, it slides up the cone shape. That makes the ice bend and then break into pieces. The smaller pieces of ice go around the pier without causing any damage at all.

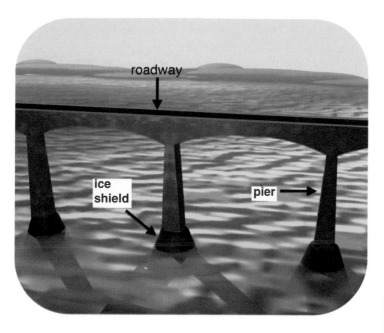

roadway

ice shield

pier

The new pier shape as well as other new design and construction ideas used on this bridge make it very special. For years to come, countries around the world will look to the Confederation Bridge for solutions to their own bridge-building challenges.

Special Concrete

The designers of the bridge had to make careful decisions about what it should be made of. They knew they needed something very strong. Steel would be strong enough against the ice and wind, but the saltwater would soon rust it and make it weak. Bridge concrete wouldn't rust, but it wasn't as strong. The bridge design team decided to use a new kind of stronger concrete, a special recipe that scientists had only previously made in laboratories.

More than 2000 men and women worked together to build the Confederation Bridge.

Other Famous Canadian Bridges

Canada's climate is so cold that Canadians have actually built bridges out of ice. In the winter of 1880–1881, and again in 1881–1882, workers built an ice bridge across the St. Lawrence River from the town of Hochelaga to Longueuil, near Montreal. From January to March, this bridge was strong enough for a small train weighing 54 432 kg to cross safely.

The Quebec Bridge

In 1900, work began to build the Quebec Bridge across the St. Lawrence River north of Quebec City. But in 1907, when the bridge was nearly finished, a large section of it twisted and fell into the river. Engineers modified the design and work began again. Then in 1916, a span that was being hoisted into place in the middle of the bridge fell into the river.

The bridge officially opened in 1919. Its early failures are famous around the world. Both accidents were studied and explained in a report that has helped engineers everywhere design better bridges.

The Lions Gate Bridge

When this bridge opened in 1938, it was the longest suspension bridge outside of the United States. It is 846 m long and took only

Quebec Bridge

Lions Gate Bridge

16 months to construct. Its towers reach a top height of 110 m above the water. The bridge stretches across Burrard Inlet and joins Vancouver with North Vancouver. An average of 61 000 vehicles cross the bridge each day.

The Hartland Covered Bridge

This bridge in Hartland, New Brunswick, crosses the St. John River. It is a special type of bridge: a covered bridge. It was built in 1899 and is 391 m long, the longest one of its kind. In the late 1800s covered bridges were quite popular, especially in eastern Canada. At that time, there were about 1000 of them in Quebec and another 400 or so in New Brunswick. The Hartland Bridge is one of only about 400 covered bridges still standing today.

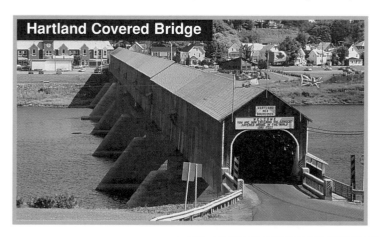

Hartland Covered Bridge

Pass the Pasta

Ever tried to make a bridge out of ... food?! Each spring for more than 10 years students in Kelowna, B.C., have been challenged to build a one-metre-long bridge using nothing but glue and 750 g (3/4 of a bag) of dry spaghetti. One winning bridge was strong enough to hold 175 kg!

AFTER YOU READ

Use headings to find the main idea

How did the headings help you to read this selection? Headings help the reader focus on the main idea of each section. Write the headings from this selection and, under each, record a sentence that tells the main idea.

I Was Born Here in This City

Written by Arnold Adoff
Illustrated by Marc Mongeau

READING TIP

Note word choice

What is your favourite building? What words would you use to describe the building and how you feel about it? As you read this poem, try to picture the buildings the poet is describing. Notice what words helped to make this picture clear for you.

I was born here in this city
but I still look up at the
magic
of tall buildings
pushing through the clouds.

One dry autumn afternoon
I lay down on the cool side-
walk in front of the downtown office tower. And all
the people had to walk
around me, because
I wouldn't stand
up until I had
seen the
clouds
move
over
the top
of that stone
giant, or the top
of that giant building
move through the clouds.

I was born here in this city
but I still look up at the
magic
of tall buildings
pushing through the clouds.

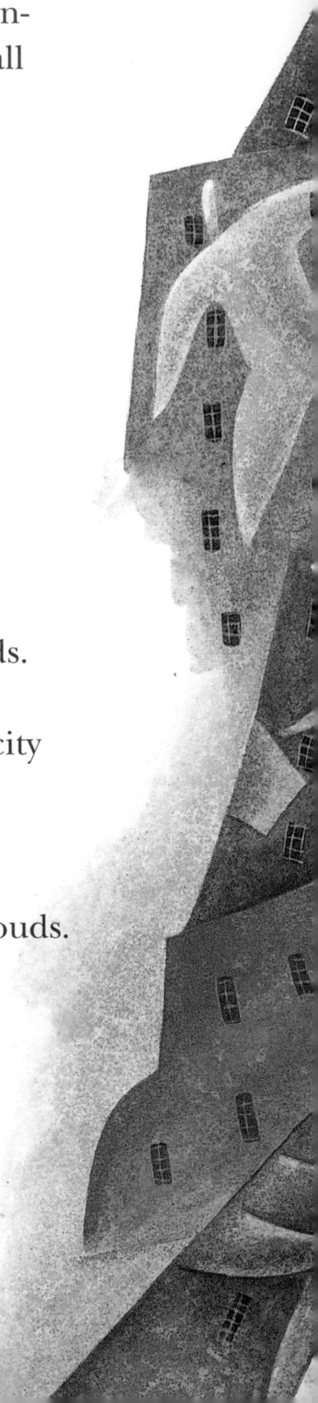

AFTER YOU READ

Write a shape or "concrete" poem

When the shape of a poem looks like what it is about, it is called a *concrete* poem. Look carefully at the shape of this poem; you might have to turn your book. Can you see the poet's buildings? Draw the outline of your building. Write a poem inside the shape using your sight and feeling words. Be sure that your words help the reader to "see" your building.

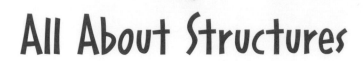

All About Structures

In this unit, you have learned about how some structures are built. You have also found out that, as well as reading words, it is also important to read graphics such as charts, diagrams and labels, floor plans, and cross sections. Now it is your turn to design a structure—your own dream home—by drawing a floor plan and writing a paragraph to describe it.

▶ Before You Begin

Think about what kind of house you would like to build. Ask yourself these questions:

- What do I already know about floor plan diagrams?
- What rooms will I want in my house?
- Where will the doors and windows be placed?
- Will it have a garage?
- Where will my house be built?
- How will I label my diagrams?
- What words will best describe my house?

Get Ideas from Other Floor Plans

- "How to Build a House," p. 84
- the real estate section of a newspaper
- home design magazines

Here is Nicola's planning chart.

Rooms	Description
Games room	- basketball court - Video games - Virtual reality
Indoor Swimming Pool	- shape of dolphin - glass roof

▶ Draw a Floor Plan

1 Make an Outline
- Decide on a shape for your house.
- Draw the outline on a sheet of paper. Graph paper works best.

2 Draw the Rooms
- Think about how the rooms will connect. Do you need a hallway to get from one room to another?
- Label your rooms clearly.

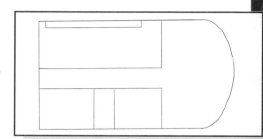

3 Use Symbols
- Diagrams do not have a lot of room for words. Use symbols to provide information.
- Think about how you will show where the features of your house are located. Be sure that the symbols you use can be understood, or use a legend to define them.

4 Add Labels
- Add any labels to your diagram that will make it easier for your reader to understand your floor plan. Labels are always printed.

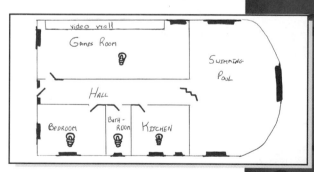

5 Add a Title

What about the furniture?

You can show where the furniture will go in each room. Here are some common shapes.

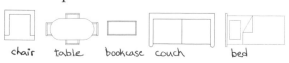

119

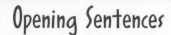

▶ Write Your First Draft

Your floor plan will give your reader a picture of the way your house is planned out. It is also useful to provide a written description of details the reader cannot see in your diagram. You might want to describe the setting for your house, the rooms, or any special features.

❶ Write an Introduction

- Write an opening sentence that catches the reader's interest.

   Here is how Nicola started her descriptive paragraph.

> Have you ever wanted to design your own house? My dream house has everything I ever wanted.

❷ Write the Body of Your Description

- Give the reader all the information they need to understand what your house looks like.

- Use words that help your reader to "see" what you are describing.

   Nicola described the special features of the games room in her house. Notice how she used words that make the reader feel as if they were in her house.

> If you describe more than one room, you will need to write a new paragraph for each room.

> The games room in my house is the size of the gym at school. It is awesome because it is full of electronics virtual reality cyberstuff along the walls. The floor is painted like a basketball court and each end of the room has a net.

❸ Write a Closing Sentence

- This part of your writing sums up the description of your house.

- Your closing sentence might tell how you feel about your house or how it is different from other houses.

▶ Put It All Together

Here are some ways you might present your floor plan and descriptive report.

- Create a poster.
- Cut out a large piece of paper in the shape of your house. Paste your floor plan and descriptive writing on it.
- Make a collage of house pictures and diagrams.

Revise and Edit

Go back and review your floor plan and your descriptive report.

- Ask a classmate or friend to read and look at your work. Are there ways to improve it?
- Did you write clear, complete sentences?
- Did you start your sentences in different ways and make them different lengths?
- Did you use size, colour, shape, and location words to describe your floor plan?
- Did you check your spelling and punctuation?
- Is your diagram neat and easy to read?
- Did you include labels and a legend to help your reader?
- Does your floor plan have a title?

Think about Your Learning

Add your own questions about what makes a good diagram and good descriptive writing.

- Did you use a web or chart to organize your ideas before you started?
- Did you draw a floor plan that was accurate and easy to read?
- Did your floor plan include labels and symbols to help your reader?
- Did you print all information on your floor plan?
- Was your descriptive writing divided into three parts—an introduction, the body, and a closing?
- Are there descriptive words in your writing to help your readers "see" the floor plan?

121

Unit 3: *In This Place*

In this unit, you will share stories and poems that Canadian authors have written about special places. Are there places that you especially like to read about? Do you have favourite *settings* (times and places) that you like to write about? As you read, think, talk, and write about the selections, you will learn how to create interesting scenes in *your own* stories and poems. You will

- read stories and poems that create word pictures of many places in Canada
- find out how authors create settings in different time periods and places
- create different kinds of poems
- give your opinions and feelings about the poems, stories, and characters you meet
- compare the stories in this unit with others you have read
- use reading strategies, such as previewing and predicting, to help you read
- write a poem and a story about a special place

Canada, My Home

READING TIP

Think about what you know

What are your ideas and feelings about Canada? Make a web with "Canada" in the centre. Add all of the words and phrases that come to mind when you think of this country. Read to see how other students feel about Canada.

Canada

To me, Canada means
bravery
and
freedom,
peace
and
joy;
Through all 10 provinces
and 3 territories
it's the best country
in the world.

Just being here
has something special
about it
with
mountains tall
and
sparkling snow
with
towering waterfalls
and
grassy meadows.
It's the best.

—*Adam Peddle, Newfoundland*

Wing Sham Leung, Ontario ↓

125

This Is Canada

Canada is a great place to be with sparkling rivers and
    deep watered seas;
With golden beaches and lakes full of leaches,
this is Canada.

Where animals can freely run,
and where rays from the sun warm up the land,
or where the juries command,
this is Canada.

This is a place where people can trust,
and hoping that nothing is left to rust,
where everyone's dreams always come true,
and the ponds are shimmering blue,
this is Canada.

This is where the days are bright,
and stay that way up to the night,
where people explore down near the ocean floor,
this is Canada.

From British C. To Newfoundland,
Canada should be known as a proud land,
and where green and vegetation grow throughout,
or wishing that people would put an end to their pouts,
only because this is Canada!

—Katie Black, Ontario

Dear Canada
Cher Canada

O Canada
great place
shocking surprise
beautiful cities
perfect mountains
O Canada
best anthem ever
great authors
quiet
gentle loving
O Canada
have peace forever
O Canada
good place

—*Nicholas Tan, British Columbia*

Maricela Quirola, Ontario ↑

If You're Not from Alberta

If you're not from Alberta,
You don't know the sunsets
You can't know the sunsets,
You can't experience the fun,
The colourful warmth in the summer,
The snowy forts in the winter
And the crowds of Klondike Days.
If you don't know Alberta,
You don't know the sunsets.

—*Jason Allman, Alberta*

127

Being a Canadian

Being a Canadian is very nice. I like being a Canadian because I have lots of friends. My family came from India. I was the only child in my family that was born in Canada. I am very proud to be a Canadian. I like the schools here. The first thing my parents saw coming here was the city of Toronto. And in Toronto, they saw the CN Tower. In Canada there are four different seasons. Every season means something different to me. In summer, I love it when it is hot and I can go swimming. In spring, I love it when the flowers start growing. It looks so beautiful. In fall, I like it when there is harvest and the leaves turn different colours. In winter, I like how the snow comes gently down and how it's so fun playing in it with your friends. Well, all I can say is that I love everything in Canada. No wonder a lot of people are moving here. And I love being a Canadian. I would never want anyone to take me to a different place. I think Canada is the best place to live.

—*Mary Thomas, Ontario*

Bonnie Tang, British Columbia ⬇

Hemon Huang, Ontario ↑

Dear Canada
Cher Canada

A beautiful place to be
With mountains, forests, and trees
Animals, oceans, and leaves
Where everybody is free
This is the place for me!
I'm proud to be Canadian!

—Geoffrey Sluggett, British Columbia

Canada, My Home

Canada, my home
Where I want to stay
Canada, my home
I love it every day
Canada, my home
Beautiful sky, beautiful sea
O wonderful Canada
Canada, my home.

—Amy Mollegaard, New Brunswick

AFTER YOU READ

Write a poem or letter

Look back at the web in which you recorded your ideas and feelings about Canada. Add any new words or ideas you thought of as you read these selections. Use your ideas to write a paragraph or poem about Canada.

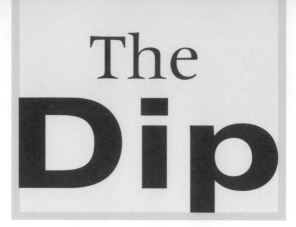

The Dip

Written by Jan Andrews
Illustrated by Paul Zwolak

READING TIP

Think about your experiences

Think about a place that is special to you. It might be a place in your home, your neighbourhood, or even a place where you go on holiday. With whom do you share your special place? How do you feel when someone new comes to your special place?

The dip was Tick Merrick's place. It was down by the abandoned beaver lodge where the stream flowed and the bare elms rose out of ferns and brush. Tick hugged the possession of it fiercely to himself, and went there often. He was glad that at last he had found a place where he did not have to screw up his small, sharp face and act tough.

But then the other kid came, and everything changed. As soon as Tick saw her, his heart sank. She was walking slowly, just as he had walked when he came to the dip for the first time. He knew that she too was looking for a place of her own.

Holding his breath, Tick ducked behind a stand of raspberry canes. Maybe if he kept still and out of sight, she would wander away and never come back. Tick bit his lip as a chipmunk squeaked at the girl. She grinned, pushed her

130

LEARNING GOALS

You will

- find out how a boy learns to share his special place

- compare your feelings and experiences to those of a character in the story

black, shaggy hair from her eyes, and settled herself comfortably against a tree trunk. Tick knew then there was no hope. The girl wouldn't go away. Springing up, he ran over to stand on the bank at the edge of the stream.

"What are you doing here? Who are you, anyhow?" he hollered.

The girl looked up, startled. "I'm Peggy," she shouted back.

"You get out," he yelled across the water at her. "You just get on out of here!"

The other kid was on her feet again in an instant. "Why?" she challenged.

"'Cause—Because it's mine here."

"Who says?"

"I do!"

Tick jumped into the stream and waded across, his small, brown eyes glowering, and his fists tight and ready. He wanted the girl to run, but she would not. Instead, she planted her feet solidly on the bank and waited for him.

"You can't be here! You can't!" Tick spat out at her.

"I can so! I can!" Peggy shot back.

The dip was spoiled for Tick after that. Every day when he went there, he and Peggy fought. They argued, called names, and threatened each other. At last, Tick declared a truce.

"OK," he called out in exasperation. "OK. You can have one side of the stream. It's—it's yours. But the right side's mine, and you keep off it. Don't you touch it, not even with a finger! You hear?" Tick received a sneering nod of reply.

Peggy kept to the agreement, but still Tick was not happy. Now he came to the dip not to enjoy it, but to guard and watch. There was no peace in it for him anymore.

Through the long summer, things went on like that. Then, one late August morning as Tick and Peggy each prowled their own sides of the stream, Tick scared a duck out of a clump of reeds. The duck hurled itself forward, limping headlong into the water. Then it flapped its wings frantically. It was trying to lift itself into the air.

"It's hurt," Peggy shouted to Tick from the other side of the stream. "It can't fly."

Peggy glanced at Tick. But before Tick could say anything, she was wading out after the fluttering bird. He was about to call out to warn her that she was crossing the invisible border line down the stream's middle. But the duck

flapped still more desperately. Tick started running.

"I'll head it off!" he cried.

"Hurry," Peggy yelled back. "I've almost got it."

The duck saw Tick and hesitated. In an instant Peggy surged forward and gathered the blur of brown-and-white feathers in her grasp. The bird writhed and twisted, almost escaping. Without thinking, Tick tore off his jacket.

"Here!" he cried as he too waded into the stream. "Give it to me. I'll wrap it in this."

Peggy handed the duck over to Tick, and a look passed between them.

"We'll—we'll take it to my side," he said.

Shivering from the cold water, they climbed the bank onto dry land. As Tick gently unwrapped his burden, Peggy's grimy hands reached toward it.

"I said it was hurt, didn't I?" she burst out.

One of the duck's wings hung limp and twisted. As Tick and Peggy looked closer, they saw that one of its legs was also bent.

"Think we could fix it?" Tick asked, narrowing his brown eyes.

"We could try," the girl said with fierce determination.

Again the look passed between them.

"We both found it, didn't we?" Tick said.

Peggy flicked at her shaggy cowlick. "Yes," she agreed.

From then on there wasn't much time for feuding. The duck took all Tick's and Peggy's attention. They bandaged its wing and made a splint for its leg. They kept it in a box and took turns having it at home at night. Together they even made a raft for the duck so that it could sit out in the stream for a few minutes, floating on the water.

Tick and Peggy watched and tenderly cared for the duck. But despite their efforts, it did not do well. Mainly, it would not eat. The carefully gathered worms and scraps of lettuce ... the bits of hamburger ... the waterweed ... all were ignored.

"It wants to die, doesn't it," Peggy said one morning as the duck huddled miserably in its box.

"I think so," Tick answered bleakly.

"I think so, too."

Peggy seemed about to say something else but changed her mind. Tick cleared his throat. He had been about to say something as well. He changed his mind, too.

The duck lived the rest of that day and into the next. Then, suddenly and quietly, it died. Tick and Peggy took the light, cold body and laid it on the raft they had made. They decorated the raft with leaves and sent it floating away. As it neared a bend in the stream, Peggy's eyes filled with tears.

"I'll go now," she said unsteadily.

Tick swallowed. "You don't have to," he answered, hunching his shoulders and jamming his hands into his pockets.

"You were here first," Peggy reminded him.

"I gave you a side of the stream, didn't I?"

"Only because I wouldn't leave."

The girl began to trudge away through dead leaves and grass.

"I *said* you could stay," Tick called after her.

Peggy turned to face him, standing small and tense and firm. "I don't want to stay if you mind," she said clearly.

"Yeah, well, I don't. I don't mind, not anymore."

"Really?"

"Really."

"OK then." Peggy headed back across the stream, climbed the bank, and sat down.

The dip was Tick Merrick's place once again. His and Peggy's. They went there often.

AFTER YOU READ

Compare your experiences

Use a diagram like this to show how your feelings and experiences with a special place are the same as or different from Tick's.

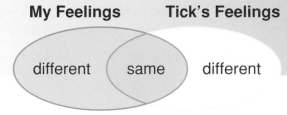

My Feelings   Tick's Feelings

different   same   different

Naomi's Road

Written by Joy Kogawa
Excerpted from the novel Naomi's Road
Illustrated by Daphne McCormack

READING TIP

Identify with the characters

This story tells about Naomi and her family who were sent to live in a small town away from the West coast during World War II because people thought they might send signals to an enemy army. As you read, think about how you would feel if someone thought you were an enemy of Canada.

The Second World War was fought by Canada and her allies against Germany and Japan. Many Canadians whose parents or grandparents had originally come from Japan were suspected, wrongly, of being enemy spies. Their homes were taken away from them by the Canadian government, and they were forced to move to remote regions of the Canadian West.

This story, from the novel Naomi's Road, *is about a girl who, with her brother Stephen, has been separated from her parents because they came from Japan. Naomi is now cared for by her aunt, whom she calls "Obasan."*

A year has passed since we came to Slocan, and a school has been built. It's half a mile away, where everyone lives in the rows and rows of huts.

The path to school is through the forest. Every school day, Stephen and I carry our lunches and school bags. For lunch I have a boiled egg and dandelion greens and Obasan's onigiri rice balls with a salty red plum in the middle. Stephen takes sandwiches and an apple or an orange.

On the way home from school, Stephen and I walk by a big white house. There's a swing in the back yard. A pretty girl about my age lives there. She has light golden hair like Goldilocks. Sometimes, before we reach her yard, we can see her swinging on her swing. Higher and higher she goes, her toes pointing up to the sky.

One day we stand at the fence and watch her.

"Boy," Stephen says. "I bet she'll go right around."

Toys are all over her back yard, like a toy store. There's a doll carriage and a doll house and a doll's tea set on a doll's table. And there are two real live white bunnies hopping in a pen. I wish I could hold the bunnies. They look as fluffy and soft as cotton wool.

The golden-haired girl sees us standing at the fence. She scrapes her feet on the ground to stop her swinging. Then she jumps off.

"What are you staring at?" she asks. She sounds angry. I want to run away into the trees. She makes a face at us and stomps her feet.

"Go away," she shouts.

What a mean girl. "Come on," I say to Stephen. I start to walk down the path.

But Stephen is angry. He whacks at the grass with his lunch pail.

"Go 'way," the girl shouts again.

"Why should I?" Stephen says. "This is a free country."

"It's not your country," the girl says.

"It is so," Stephen says.

"It is not," she shouts.

A red and white checked curtain in the window behind her moves. There's a woman who also has golden hair, looking out at us. She raps on the window with her knuckles. The girl looks back. The woman is shaking her head.

❖ ❖ ❖ ❖ ❖ ❖ ❖ ❖ ❖ ❖ ❖ ❖ ❖ ❖ ❖

"I can't play with you," the girl says in a sing-song voice. She points her chin to the sky and turns her head.

I run through the trees, taking a short cut away from the path. The thick pine-needle floor crackles as I go. I can hear Stephen behind me hitting the trees with his lunch pail.

I don't like the horrid girl. I don't like walking by her house. I don't like school either. In the morning I don't like having my hair combed. My hair is getting long and Obasan braids it in pigtails. I don't like my pigtails.

But I like climbing the mountains. I like playing with my Mickey Mouse who can walk by itself down a slope. I like reading my grade-three reader and Stephen's grade-five reader. And I like reading the comics in the newspaper.

There are some funny roly-poly comic-strip boys called the Katzenjammer Kids. They play tricks on a mean little rich boy called Rollo. And there's a fuzzy-haired girl with empty-circle eyes called Little Orphan Annie. She is always saved from danger by her Daddy Warbucks. Sometimes I lie in my bunk bed at night pretending I'm Little Orphan Annie being rescued by my Daddy.

Stephen likes to read the comics too. But he also reads the harder parts of the newspaper. He says he has to know what's happening in the war. Uncle and Stephen talk about the war together while they chop wood.

One day Stephen comes running home with a red, white, and blue Union Jack. It's the same as the flag high up on a pole at school. He holds it high in the air and the flag flaps behind him.

"Where did you get that?" I ask.

"I won it," Stephen says. "I traded it for all my marbles." Back and forth he waves the flag. Then he nails it to a long pole and plants it in a hole at the top of Uncle's rock garden. The flag hangs quietly and peacefully high up in the air.

When Stephen jumps back down again, he stands at attention facing the flag. Then he salutes it.

"We have to sing 'God Save the King,'" Stephen says. He makes a trumpet out of his hands. After that we sing "Land of Hope and Glory" and "O Canada." When we are singing "Hearts of Oak," I see the horrid girl walking up the path.

We stop. She stops, too. She's staring at us and staring at the flag.

"That's not your flag," she says.

"It is too," Stephen says.

"You stole it," she shouts. "Give it to me."

"It's mine," Stephen shouts back.

"You're going to lose the war," she says in her sing-song voice.

"We will NOT!" Stephen yells so loud I cover my ears and run into the house.

From inside the house Obasan and I listen to Stephen pounding on the tub drum. Obasan's eyes are shut.

❖ ❖ ❖ ❖ ❖ ❖ ❖ ❖ ❖ ❖ ❖ ❖ ❖ ❖

After a while Stephen comes in and climbs into his bunk. He lies down and takes the flute from under his pillow. All the songs he can remember, he plays and plays and plays. Even when it's time to sleep he keeps playing. Uncle joins in with the tappity-tappity sounds of spoons on his knees.

"Good music," Uncle says to Stephen.

"Good drumming, Uncle," Stephen replies.

When Nomura-obasan was with us, she used to say, "Music will heal us all." Obasan says it now, quietly, with her eyes closed.

AFTER YOU READ

Tell about the characters

Make a chart like this to tell your opinions about the three children in the story: Naomi, Stephen, and the blonde girl.

Character	My Opinion or Reaction	My Reasons
Naomi		
Stephen		
Blonde girl		

Josepha:

A Prairie Boy's Story

Written by Jim McGugan
Illustrated by Murray Kimber

READING TIP

Look for clues about setting

The setting of a story is when and where the story takes place. Writers do not always tell you exactly when a story takes place. As you read, look for clues that the author gives you about when this story took place.

It was late in the last afternoon, long after the school bell, when I made good-byes to Josepha.

Prairie wind ruffled his hair. Barefoot, he stood silent and still as a Saturday flagpole. The sun flickered between leaves in the windbreak poplars, licking his face in shadow and light. Shadow and light. And a farm cart's four wheels groaned and whined not far down the gravel track. A farm cart coming for Josepha.

142

143

Over the beating of my heart, I could hear them plain, drumming and churning inside my head. Josepha hummed the wagon's tune. He growled louder and louder as the wagon grew nearer and nearer. Then his eyes watered, and his breath gave out. And he coughed and laughed. And I laughed, too.

I tried to stretch up and clutch Josepha's elbow, but he broke free. And he reeled around me, clapping the grey dirt walk. Smacking the land with the soles of his naked feet. Wee slaps bouncing up from the ground, like the whack of Josepha's twine suspenders plucking against his bare back.

Rap rap tap. Josepha's slate oftimes slipped onto the pine plank floor. Our schoolhouse floor. The floor way over in primary row. *Rap rap tap.* Red-faced Josepha. Past fourteen and trying to learn in primary row.

"Please, Josepha," Miss said. "Say it again."

To the newcomers, our words must have sounded like sheep talk. The younger children might fight to understand, but the older ones, never. When they braved to speak, they were made the fool.

As always, Josepha bore teasing with a smile. That last winter, though, someone dared to mock his sister. He reeled, then faced the class. I could smell his rage, and I was scared. Josepha quivered. But he could not say what he had to say.

He did not know how.

Later, Josepha wept. Miss sat by him until home time, resting her hand on his shoulder.

English speaking was the rule. Talk in English. Print in English. Think in English. Or sit with the little ones till you're able.

So silent Josepha sat with me.

And became my friend *for aye*, for always.

All hushed and muffled like a frozen river. A blushing bull in primary row. His final year in primary row.

Josepha could never suffer older boys' bullying. Nobody bullied us younger ones, not with Josepha standing close. And he taught me stones could fly. Clear across the marsh, if my aim was sure. I was his partner in the barrow race.

One snowy night, he tramped straight over to our section. Snowing and bitter sharp, yet he tramped to our farm and back, his feet wrapped in burlap sacking. And still Josepha laughed. He laughed like it was nothing when he gave Ma the poultice, herbs to soothe my aching ear.

And now he tramped the land again. Tramping the land with the bare soles of his feet.

"Dollar day. Dollar day. Dollar day a *baggink*."

He twirled about his sisters, jostling and jolting, jostling and jolting because that's what you do. That's what you do if you have to laugh. Jostling and jolting and rustling up clouds.

Yard dust powdered my boots, my brown boots with newspaper stuffed in the toes. They cost. They cost so much I didn't dare wear them except for very special times. Far too big and all, they were still the proudest thing I ever owned. And Josepha knew. When he saw the grit, his blue fold hankie rubbed and rubbed. And soon their leather toes shined again as bright as a birthday copper while I twitched and fussed, embarrassed.

Something dropped from his overall bib and lay tucked in the dirt.

A knife. Josepha's pocketknife. Josepha opened the blade and blew on the steel and returned it to its slot. He spun the handle around in place. One side goose-egg white, the other bare, its covering lost or broken. But the metal gleamed. He turned his knife over and over. I remembered whistles he'd carved. And I remembered dolls he'd given the littlest ones and arrows and bows for recess games. He spun the knife round and round.

Then jostling and jolting once more, he bumped into Miss. Our teacher. She made Josepha stop. And she asked him again.

"Please. Stay. Won't you stay, Josepha?"

She said his mind was soil rich and set to open. Like a flower to the sun, she said. She vowed he could learn. Come back after threshing, she said.

But Josepha's face darkened. Lightless as the window in his family's sod shack just after milking. You saw their home when you passed by at night from selling grain in town. A lonesome soddy standing on the rise, wee and frail and blackened. Supper in the gloom to save kerosene. Until next harvest. Or next. Pa said their storehouse was nothing but empty. And not a wonder, Pa said. For Josepha was the bairn of city folk, a main street shopkeeper's son. And Pa said Old Country or no, shopkeepers didn't make farmers. Farmers made farmers.

Josepha studied his teacher's eyes. He peered deep, his brow furrowing as if he were lost. Josepha sighed, then suddenly laughing, he said:

"Is dollar a day, Miss. *Baggink.*"

Eaton catalogue English, we called it. Language enough for bagging grain through threshing time. Language enough to earn a one-dollar wage.

He smiled and pried ajar the lid of his biscuit tin. A meal pail for toting his boiled potatoes to school.

From inside he offered up a violin—a doll violin the span of a tanner's hand, whittled from a single shoot of cottonwood.

"For you, Miss. Is for you."

The gingham shoulders on Miss's dress sagged a mite before she stirred. She reached to accept her gift. But Josepha drew it back. He flashed his knife. In a glint, the blade pared the slightest burr from the neck of the violin.

And he placed the toy like a day-old chick into our teacher's hand.

She realized the work and wanted to protest, but didn't dare. To Josepha, a present offered must be taken.

Josepha's eldest brother reined his wagon at the gate. Miss rubbed along the smoothness on the back of the violin with the edge of her thumb. She glared, angrily watching the old plow horse shake its leathers. The animal snorted, gnawing heads off some soft purple chicory clustered near the posts. And Miss brushed her thumb round and round and said:

"It is nineteen hundred. Nineteen hundred, Josepha. A fresh century in your chosen land. You are quick and bright and cunning. Oh, the wealth of knowing you could reap."

Josepha shrugged. Sheep talk. And Miss sighed.

This was the way for all of them, those older ones. One year, shamed. Maybe two. And then they'd be gone from class. They'd be gone forever.

"Best fortune, Josepha," Miss said. Then turning like a weather vane in a firebolt sky, she marched back to her empty school.

Josepha upped his sisters into the wagon.

And my forehead heated to a fever.

A gift. I could not think. I wanted to offer a gift to Josepha. A gift of his own for all the marvels he had given us. The wonders he had given me. I wanted to take his hand again. I wanted to beg.

Don't be quitting school, Josepha.

Instead, I watched him spring like a ram up alongside his brother in the cart.

He squeezed a buckboard sliver from his heel, then tossed down one last favour. Startled, I pressed his knife firmly to my chest.

"Josepha. Josepha, I've a thing to give as well." And so it was.

With a "Hrup, hup!" they were gone. Josepha shrinking smaller and smaller in the dust. And by the fork, he vanished into a hazy puff. Alone, I crossed the fallows home. I clutched the knife inside my fist. I wrung it greedily for memories.

Late in the last afternoon, trudging home.

Barefoot and pondering on Josepha.

AFTER YOU READ

Find evidence

When do you think the story took place? List all of the clues from the story that support your opinion.

In My Back Yard

Illustrated by Joe Biafore

Silence
and a deeper silence
when the crickets
hesitate

Leonard Cohen

Soft rain greening
The city
A robin shouting

Elizabeth Kouhi

152

River at twilight:
I watch the darkness flow
into my eyes

George Swede

With my fidgeting
fingernails beside white waves
I crumble sandstone.

Milton Acorn

AFTER YOU READ

Write a poem

A *haiku* is a short poem, usually three lines in length, that describes something in nature. Think about a place that is special to you. What words and ideas describe your place? Your poem will be very short, so choose your words carefully to give your reader a good mind picture. Now shape your ideas into a haiku.

THE
First Red Maple Leaf

Written and illustrated by Ludmila Zeman

READING TIP

Find out about legends

Long ago, people told stories to try to explain how things in the world came to be. These stories are called legends. Think of *legends* that you already know. What do they explain? As you read, find out what this legend explains.

I left Europe as a refugee. At the airport my children asked, "Mom, which one is our airplane?"

I replied, "The one with the big red maple leaf painted on it."

When we reached Canada, the big red maple leaf was everywhere. My children said, "There were maple leaves at home. Why is the maple leaf the symbol of Canada?" I did not know.

But one day, we went for a walk in the woods and the maple leaves were falling all around us, each red leaf so large that a child could find shelter under it. So this is the story I told my children about the big red maple leaf.

❖ ❖ ❖ ❖ ❖

154

Long ago when the world was young and raw, the people knew nothing but winter. Whichever way they turned, Iceheart lay in wait for them. His breath whined like the wind, and the sound of his gnashing teeth was like icicles snapping. He gripped them in his freezing claws and the breath died in their throats. They went east, and there was Iceheart, waiting. They turned north, and Iceheart rose up before them. They fled west, and Iceheart overtook them.

The very earth moaned in the cold, and the trees sighed and fell whenever Iceheart breathed upon them.

As one tree dropped frozen and dead in the snow, Branta the goose lay trapped beneath it. A child of the people ran to gather up the goose thinking, "Here is food," but Branta cried, "Spare my life and I will lead you to safety." Then the boy set the goose free. Iceheart watched with angry eyes.

The grey goose flew first at Iceheart, covering his eyes until the boy fled. Then she flew south, calling, "People, follow me."

So the people ran south where the goose had led them, and at last they came upon a forest of tall trees, with leaves as red as the setting sun.

Iceheart followed the people south in silent rage, and when they felt his frozen breath, the people hid among the trees. Iceheart tore at the trees with claw and fang, but the trees stood firm and sheltered the people. The red leaves fell so thickly that Iceheart was blinded and turned away.

The people said to one another, "We must stay here among the trees with red leaves that shelter us." But when they looked, they saw that all the red leaves lay deep on the earth like a warm blanket. Iceheart had left the trees beaten and bruised, shivering and bare. Then the boy said, "The trees saved us. We must save the trees. I will go where Branta the goose has gone. She helped us. Maybe she will help the trees."

So he climbed onto the back of a moose, and set out southward after Branta.

It was a long, daring journey through howling winds and blowing snow, but at last the boy and the great moose came to a land where the air was mild, and Iceheart was left far behind. There, swimming in a lake with her goslings, was Branta the goose.

The boy said, "Oh, Branta, I have come to thank you for leading my people to safety. We hid among trees that

gave up their leaves to hide us and shelter us. May I ask your help again? How can we save the trees?"

Branta the goose said, "Leave your friend here to rest and mind my children, and climb up on my back." And, with the boy on her back, Branta the goose flew south toward the sun.

At last they came to a land more beautiful and full of colour than the boy had ever seen, a land where the trees were always green and so filled with bright, singing birds that the boy could not tell birds from leaves. Branta the goose called the birds to her and told them of the trees in the north that had lost their leaves.

Then it seemed to the boy that the leaves took to the air and followed the goose as she flew north once more, bringing summer behind her. When they came to the forest where the trees stood, the birds alighted on the bare branches, covering them with their beautiful colours. No matter how hard Iceheart blew his frosty winds, grateful people found shelter. Defeated, Iceheart fled before glorious summer.

"But we cannot stay here always," said Branta the goose. "In winter we must fly south once more, but never fear, for all time winter and summer will take turns and the leaves will always come again."

◆　◆　◆　◆　◆

Whatever the season, the red maple leaf shelters my new country. For me, it represents the sense of safety I felt when I first came here with my family.

AFTER YOU READ

Write your own legend

Pick another Canadian symbol such as the Canada goose, the beaver, or hockey. Write your own legend about how this symbol came to be. Use "The First Red Maple Leaf" and other legends you know as models to help you write.

Akla Gives Chase

Written by James Houston
Illustrated by Robert Johannsen

READING TIP

Make predictions

When you read a long story, it is especially important to set the scene for yourself at the beginning. Look at the title and the illustrations. Read the opening paragraphs slowly and carefully. Try to visualize the scene and the characters. Think about what might happen. Now, you're ready to read on!

Upik and Pitohok are two Inuit children whose father has died. Now they must fetch food for the rest of the family, or starve. The previous autumn, their grandfather shot a caribou which he was unable to carry home, but left hidden. It is a long journey to the hiding place, but the children are the only hope of their mother, their two baby sisters, and their grandfather. They find the caribou, but on the long journey home they are pursued by Long Claws, or akla—a grizzly bear that is hungry, too.

Together they hurried away, trying to hide themselves from Long Claws in the heavy ice fog. They walked and walked until they came to a riverbed that seemed familiar to them. Violent winds had blown one bank free of snow, but in the swirling fog they could not tell where it would lead them. Pitohok struggled up onto the stones that formed the bank of the frozen river. His sister had to help him by pushing at his back.

LEARNING GOALS

You will

- read an adventure story about two children on a dangerous journey in northern Canada

- make predictions about a story

- explain your ideas and feelings about events in a story

159

"Be careful not to leave a single track up here," Pitohok gasped. "Step from rock to rock," he warned her. "The wind is at our back. If the akla cannot see us or smell our footprints, we may lose him."

Together they travelled on the stony riverbank until about midday, following a twisted course, leaving no path behind them.

"I hope we are far enough away from him," Pitohok gasped. "I can walk no farther."

He sank to his knees and let the heavy weight of the caribou sag down until it rested on the wind-cleared stones. He lay against it, his chest heaving as he tried to catch his breath. Although the air was stinging cold, Upik had to kneel and wipe the frost-white sweat from her brother's face.

"He's gone." Upik sighed, glad to rest the heavy rifle in the snow. She looked around in the still-thick fog. "Which way do we go now?"

Pitohok peered over his shoulder and felt cold sweat trickling down his spine. He could see no sign of the sun. Everything was hidden by a wall of fog.

"I ... I don't know," he admitted. "I was trying so hard to get away from the akla that now ... we're lost!"

Pitohok struggled painfully onto his knees and looked in all directions. He saw nothing but grey ice fog that drifted in phantom swirls along the frozen river.

"Oh, I wish someone would help us," Upik whispered aloud, and as if in answer to her words, the snowy owl came toward her, winging low out of the fog. Upik saw the owl turn its head as though it had seen the bear, then stare at her with its huge golden-yellow eyes. Suddenly the owl changed its wingbeat, hovering as if by magic at the very edge of the smokelike mists. It seemed to signal Upik. Then, turning sharply to the right, it flew off, cutting a dark trail through the ice-cold wall of fog.

Upik stood up, and, using all her strength, helped her brother heave the caribou onto his back. She struggled to ease the heavy burden as she stood upright.

"We should follow her," said Upik. "I think she knows the way."

Her brother's answer was a moan when the full weight of the frozen caribou settled on his tired, cramped shoulders. "Yes, follow the owl," he whispered.

Upik tried to steady Pitohok while they walked. She looked back only once at the zigzag trail they left in the snow as her brother's strength grew less and less. Both of them had lost all sense of distance and of time. Upik followed the owl's course through the dense fog, wondering if they would ever reach their home.

They had not gone far before Upik heard the sound of heavy breathing. She turned, then screamed in terror. The huge grizzly, its heavy head rolling, its tongue lolling out of its mouth, came padding after them. It was only a pace behind Pitohok. Upik saw Long Claws raise its head and sniff at the rich burden of caribou, which had softened a little because of the heat of Pitohok's body. The grizzly stretched out its neck and licked the frosted nostrils of the caribou.

"What's the matter?" Pitohok asked her. Then turning, he, too, saw the bear. His voice caught in his throat. "You've got to ... to try and shoot him," Pitohok gasped. "I can't do it. My arms are too tired. My whole body is trembling from carrying this weight. Let him get close to you," he said, "then shoot him ... in the head."

Upik stopped, raised the heavy rifle, and tried to sight along its wavering barrel. "I can't," she said. "I am afraid ... afraid this last stone bullet will break." She was weeping. "Drop the caribou," Upik begged her brother. "Let Long Claws take it. We can walk away alive. It will stop and eat. Please drop the caribou. I am afraid that the akla is going to kill you for that meat."

Pitohok hunched his shoulders and struggled forward, as if he had not heard her plea. But now Upik could see that he held his short knife in his hand and that he would not give up their prize of meat without a fight.

Once more she heard an angry rumble in the grizzly's throat and saw it reach out with one terrible paw and rake the caribou along the whole length of its back. As its claws hooked against the caribou's antlers, Pitohok was thrown off balance and stumbled sideways, falling onto his knees. The big bear moved closer. Driven by fear and desperation, Pitohok rose and continued walking, his eyes narrowed, his mouth drawn down with strain.

The huge akla, with lips drawn back to show its enormous teeth, came after him again. Upik once more raised her grandfather's rifle and looked along its sights. The bear must have heard the safety catch click off, for it stopped, turned its head, and stared straight up the gun barrel at her. At that moment, looking into its eyes, Upik realized that the bear was neither good nor evil. It

was a hunter like themselves, desperate to feed itself and remain alive in the lonely, snow-filled wilderness. She lowered the rifle. She could not bring herself to try to kill the bear.

At that moment, Pitohok whispered hoarsely, "I see the owl again! She's sitting on our family's empty food cache. Can it be?" he sobbed. "Are we ... almost home?"

The bear moved in again behind him and, rising up on its hind feet, struck out angrily at the caribou's plump haunches. Pitohok reeled from the heavy blow and staggered to his knees. He tried to rise, then sank back onto the snow.

"I can't go on," he said. "I'm finished." He had lost his knife. There were tears in his eyes, but his teeth were clenched in anger. He tightened his grip upon the caribou.

"Let go," Upik begged her brother. "Let him have the meat."

"No," Pitohok said. "If I lose this caribou to that bear and return home with nothing, none of us will live, and I, myself, would die of shame."

He turned away from the hot breath of the snarling grizzly whose great swaying head was not more than an arm's length from his face.

"Run!" Pitohok whispered to his sister. "Run for the igloo and save yourself."

Upik bent and grabbed her brother underneath the arms, trying to help him up, but he was too weak. Then she turned around so that she stood directly between him and the akla's gaping jaws.

"No—don't do that," Pitohok gasped. He was hunched over like an old man. "Put the rifle under the caribou to help me support this weight," he moaned, "or I ... shall never rise. You run!" he begged his sister. Pitohok wept aloud as he whispered, "I can't do any more. All my strength has gone. It's going black ... I'm going to ...."

"You are coming with me, now!" cried Upik. "I can see our igloo. It's not far from us. Can you not see it through the fog?"

The big grizzly raked its claws through the snow. Upik put her left shoulder underneath the caribou and her arm around her brother's waist and strained with all her might. Together they rose from the snow and staggered off toward their family's house. Pitohok stumbled once again and fell onto one knee. He hung there gasping for breath.

The akla snarled and opened its mouth wide to take the caribou's leg and Pitohok's mitted hand between its crushing jaws.

"*Unalook! Kukikotak!*" Upik screamed at the bear. "We shared our fish with you. Don't you dare to harm my brother. He must take this food home to our family. They are starving ... don't you understand?"

The huge bear let go of Pitohok's hand and the caribou's leg and stood there glaring back at her.

"Quick! Get back on your feet," Upik whispered. "We have only a little way to go."

The grizzly must have seen the snowhouse, too, for suddenly it shambled around in front of them, blocking Pitohok's way.

"I warned you not to hurt my brother," Upik screamed again.

As if ruled by magic, the huge bear stepped back and let them pass.

"Mother! Mother! Come and help us!" Upik wailed.

Long Claws turned its head and stared at her when Upik's mother burst out of their igloo entrance. She saw the great humped shoulders of the akla and, like her daughter, screamed at it, then turned and rushed inside again.

Upik tried to take half of the caribou's weight on her own shoulders while pulling Pitohok to his feet. Slowly he rose, but his knees would scarcely support him.

"Don't drop it now," Upik said in a stern voice. "We're almost there."

Together they staggered painfully toward the igloo.

"Everything is whirling around," cried Pitohok. "It's going black again ... I'm falling...."

Because she no longer had the strength to hold him, Upik and her brother collapsed together on the snow. She shook him, but Pitohok seemed to have lost the power to hear or move or speak. Upik tried to drag him toward the igloo, but his arms remained locked tight around their precious burden of meat.

Long Claws turned once more and shambled after them, snarling like a huge and angry dog. It grasped the caribou's neck in its powerful jaws and started backing away, dragging the carcass and Pitohok, pulling both of them into the swirling fog.

166

The snow knife, the rifle, and Pitohok's short knife were gone. Upik had no weapons but her hands and teeth. She turned and saw her grandfather crawling out of the igloo on his hands and knees. In his left mitt he held his huge curved bow and in his mouth a pair of arrows. Right behind him came their mother, her parka hood puffed out with icy wind, screaming aloud, raging to protect her children, ready to do battle with the enormous bear. Her hands outstretched like claws, their mother raced forward to attack.

Upik heard her grandfather call out, "Stop, woman. Hold! If you help me, we can pierce him right from here."

The grandfather knelt unsteadily and notched an arrow to the braided string. His hands shook with strain when he tried to draw the powerful bow. But he could not. In desperation Upik's mother knelt and helped to draw the heavy weapon almost to full curve. The point of the arrow wavered wildly when the grandfather tried to aim.

"Don't!" Upik cried, spreading her arms and running between her grandfather's unsteady arrow and the bear. "You might hit Pitohok."

Looking back, she saw her brother still being dragged across the snow behind the bear. In sudden anger she whirled around and ran straight between her brother and the akla, screaming, *You let go of him! Let go!*

Surprised, the huge grizzly released the caribou for a moment and raised its head.

"Here, this is for you," she yelled and reaching into her parka hood, she snatched out the last piece of frozen trout that she had saved and flung it beyond the bear.

The akla looked at her, grunted, then turned and moved away from Pitohok, who still clasped the caribou as fiercely as an Arctic crab. The grizzly snatched up the piece of fish. Then, with its hips and frosted shoulders rolling, it disappeared into the silver wall of icy fog.

Pitohok's mother and his grandfather knelt beside him, trying to unlock his arms from the caribou.

Pitohok opened his eyes and stared at them. "I thought that akla would surely snatch the caribou away from me," he whispered.

"I, too, believed that he would take it from you," his grandfather agreed. "But no human knows exactly what the animals will do."

"Upik was afraid of the akla. We were both afraid of him, and yet she ran and put her body between me and the grizzly's snarling jaws. Grandfather, did you believe my sister would do that?"

"No. I did not know what she would do. Nobody knows the strength or courage that humans possess until real danger comes to test them."

• •

AFTER YOU READ

Explain your reactions

Choose three parts of the story that stand out in your mind. For each part, tell how it made you feel and explain why.

When ... I felt ... because ...

Picture T·H·I·S

READING TIP

Make a personal response

Think about poems you have read and heard. What kinds of poems do you usually like? Jot down two or three ideas about what makes a poem interesting or appealing to you.

In the Wet Haze

The house is locked, the roof is done.
I stop my pounding, gather up my tools
and stare. In the wet haze
a great blue heron slides west
a single line of smoke in the evening air.

Patrick Lane

I Am

In this house, in this tree,
　　On this old vacant lot,
In this place where I am
　　And my brother is not,
The biggest and bravest,
　　The strongest and boldest,
The shrewdest and smartest,
　　The wisest and oldest.
In my house, in my tree,
　　In my own special spot,
In this place where I am
　　And my brother is not.

Marilyn Helmer

January in Suburban Windsor

The hibachi
left outside for the winter
is cooking up a nice thick
hamburger of snow.

Tom Wayman

pender street east

fresh rock cod
a pleasant smile
roast pork fresh hot
taste before you buy
(guarantee to satisfy)
ginger green onions
soy sauce   msg

take a break
across the street
find a booth
order green tea
relax ...
where else would you possibly
want to be?

Jim Wong-Chu

Ice

Ice
builds up.

Wind badgers the maples.

Something's
got to
give.

Gary Geddes

River

Sitting by the river
listening to the waterfalls
rapids singing as
water flows along the river
feeling the peacefulness
as you listen to the rapids
  singing.

Breeze blowing gently
listening to the rustling
leaves up in the trees
birds singing in the distance.

Hearing a lone loon
somewhere on the distant lake
listening to his sad
lonely haunting sound.

Little animals come to the
river to drink

Looking up in clear blue sky
eagles circling peacefully
searching for their prey.

It saddens you
to leave the peacefulness
by the riverside
rapids singing as
water flows along the river.

Back to the noisy city
listening to the cars, buses, trains
no more peacefulness
no more listening to the rapids
  singing
as water flows down the river.
As water flows down the river.

Archie Toulouse

173

And my heart soars

The beauty of the trees,
the softness of the air,
the fragrance of the grass,
     speaks to me.

The summit of the mountain,
the thunder of the sky,
the rhythm of the sea,
     speaks to me.

The faintness of the stars,
the freshness of the morning,
the dew drop on the flower,
     speaks to me.

The strength of fire,
the taste of salmon,
the trail of the sun,
And the life that never goes away,
     They speak to me.

And my heart soars.

Chief Dan George

rush hour in the rain

wet streets
shiny black like licorice
twisting through the city

traffic tastes its way home.

Tiffany Stone

AFTER YOU READ

Explain your preferences

Choose one of the poems in this section that you especially liked.
Write a short paragraph explaining what you liked about it.

On Island Rock

Written by L. M. Montgomery
Illustrated by Paul McCusker

READING TIP

Think about what you know

Think about animal heroes that you know about from other stories. What heroic deeds did they do? Did the setting of the stories play an important part? Make a list of some common features in animal hero stories. As you read, see how many of these features are used in this story.

"Who was the man I saw talking to you in the hayfield?" asked Aunt Kate, as Uncle Richard came in to dinner.

"Bob Marks," said Uncle Richard briefly. "I've sold Laddie to him."

Ernest Hughes, the twelve-year-old orphan boy whom Uncle "boarded and kept" for the chores he did, suddenly stopped eating.

"Oh, Mr. Lawson, you're not going to sell Laddie?" he cried chokily.

Uncle Richard stared at him. Never before, in the five years that Ernest had lived with him, had the quiet little fellow spoken without being spoken to, much less ventured to protest against anything Uncle Richard might do.

176

LEARNING GOALS

You will

- read a story about an animal hero

- use what you know about other stories to help you read this one

"Certainly I am," answered the latter curtly. "Bob offered me twenty dollars for the dog, and he's coming after him next week."

"Oh, Mr. Lawson," said Ernest, rising to his feet, his small, freckled face crimson. "Oh, don't sell Laddie! *Please*, Mr. Lawson, don't sell him!"

"What nonsense is this?" said Uncle Richard sharply.

He was a man who never changed his mind when it was once made up.

"Don't sell Laddie!" pleaded Ernest miserably. "He is the only friend I've got. I can't live if Laddie goes away. Oh, don't sell him, Mr. Lawson!"

"Sit down and hold your tongue," said Uncle Richard sternly. "The dog is mine, and I shall do with him as I think

177

fit. He is sold, and that is all there is about it. Go on with your dinner."

But Ernest for the first time did not obey. He snatched his cap from the back of his chair, dashed it down over his eyes, and ran from the kitchen with a sob choking his breath. Uncle Richard looked angry, but Aunt Kate hastened to soothe him.

"Don't be vexed with the boy, Richard," she said. "You know he is very fond of Laddie. He's had to do with him ever since he was a pup, and no doubt he feels badly at the thought of losing him. I'm rather sorry myself that you have sold the dog."

"Well, he *is* sold and there's an end of it. I don't say but that the dog is a good dog. But he is of no use to us, and twenty dollars will come in mighty handy just now. He's worth that to Bob, for he is a good watchdog, so we've both made a fair bargain."

Nothing more was said about Ernest or Laddie.

I was spending my vacation at Uncle Richard's farm on the Nova Scotian Bay of Fundy shore. I was a great favourite with Uncle Richard, partly because he had been much attached to my mother, his only sister, partly because of my strong resemblance to his only son, who had died several years before. Uncle Richard was a stern man, but I knew that he entertained a deep and real affection for me, and I always enjoyed my vacations at his place.

"What are you going to do this afternoon, Ned?" he asked, after the disturbance caused by Ernest's outbreak had quieted down.

"I think I'll row out to Island Rock," I replied. "I want to take some views of the shore from it."

Uncle Richard nodded. He was much interested in my new camera.

"If you're on it about four o'clock, you'll get a fine view of the 'Hole in the Wall' when the sun begins to shine on the water through it," he said. "I've often thought it would make a handsome picture."

"After I've finished taking the pictures, I think I'll go down shore to Uncle Adam's and stay all night," I said. "Jim's darkroom is more convenient than mine, and he has some pictures he is going to develop tonight, too."

I started for the shore about two o'clock. Ernest was sitting on the woodpile as I passed through the yard, with his arms about Laddie's neck and his face buried in Laddie's curly hair. Laddie was a handsome and intelligent black-and-white Newfoundland, with a magnificent coat. He and Ernest were great chums. I felt sorry for the boy who was to lose his pet.

"Don't take it so hard, Ern," I said, trying to comfort him. "Uncle will likely get another pup."

"I don't want any other pup!" Ernest blurted out. "Oh, Ned, won't you try and coax your uncle not to sell him?

Perhaps he'd listen to you."

I shook my head. I knew Uncle Richard too well to hope that.

"Not in this case, Ern," I said. "He would say it did not concern me, and you know nothing moves him when he determines on a thing. You'll have to reconcile yourself to losing Laddie, I'm afraid."

Ernest's tow-coloured head went down on Laddie's neck again, and I, deciding that there was no use in saying anything more, proceeded toward the shore, which was about two kilometres from Uncle Richard's house. About three hundred metres from the shore was the peculiar formation known as Island Rock. This was a large rock that stood abruptly up out of the water. Below, about the usual water line, it was seamed and fissured, but its summit rose up in a narrow, flat-topped peak. At low tide six metres of it was above water, but at high tide it was two metres and often more under water.

I pushed Uncle Richard's small flat down the rough path and rowed out to Island Rock. Arriving there, I thrust the painter deep into a narrow cleft. This was the usual way of mooring it, and no doubt of its safety occurred to me.

I scrambled up the rock and around to the eastern end, where there was a broader space for standing and from which some capital views could be obtained. The sea about the rock was calm, but there was quite a swell on and an offshore breeze was blowing. There were no boats visible. The tide was low, leaving bare the curious caves and headlands along shore, and I secured a number of excellent snapshots. It was now three o'clock. I must wait another hour yet before I could get the best view of the "Hole in the Wall"—a huge, arch-like opening through a jutting headland to the west of me. I went around to look at it, when I saw a sight that made me stop short in dismay. This was nothing less than the flat, drifting outward around the point. The swell and suction of the water around the rock must have pulled her loose—and I was a prisoner! At first my only feeling was one of annoyance. Then a thought flashed into my mind that made me dizzy with fear. The tide would be high that night. If I could not escape from Island Rock I would inevitably be drowned.

I sat down limply on a ledge and tried to look matters fairly in the face. I could not swim; calls for help could not reach anybody, my only hope lay in the chance of somebody passing down the shore or of some boat appearing.

I looked at my watch. It was a quarter past three. The tide would begin to turn about five, but it would be at least ten before the rock would be covered. I had, then, little more than six hours to live unless rescued.

I have heard of time seeming long to a person in my predicament, but to me it seemed fairly to fly, for every moment decreased my chance of rescue. I determined I would not give way to cowardly fear, so, with a murmured prayer for help, I set myself to the task of waiting for death as bravely as possible. At intervals I shouted as loudly as I could and, when the sun came to the proper angle for the best view of the "Hole in the Wall," I took the picture. It afterward turned out to be a great success, but I have never been able to look at it without a shudder.

At five the tide began to come in. Very, very slowly the water rose around Island Rock. Up, up, up it came, while I watched it with fascinated eyes, feeling like a rat in a trap. The sun fell lower and lower: at eight o'clock the moon rose large and bright; at nine it was a lovely night, clear, calm, bright as day, and the water was swishing over the highest ledge of the rock. With some difficulty I climbed to the top and sat there to await the end. I had no longer any hope of rescue but, by a great effort, I preserved self-control. If I had to die, I would at least face death staunchly. But when I thought of my mother at home, it tasked all my energies to keep from breaking down utterly.

Suddenly I heard a whistle. Never was sound so sweet. I stood up and peered eagerly shoreward. Coming around the "Hole in the Wall" headland, on top of the cliffs, I saw a boy and a dog. I sent a wild halloo ringing shoreward.

The boy started, stopped, and looked out toward
Island Rock. The next moment he hailed me. It was Ernest's
voice, and it was Laddie who was barking beside him.

"Ernest," I shouted wildly, "run for help—quick! quick!
The tide will be over the rock in half an hour! Hurry, or you
will be too late!"

Instead of starting off at full speed as I expected him to
do, Ernest stood still for a moment and then began to pick
his steps down a narrow path over the cliff, followed by
Laddie.

"Ernest," I shouted frantically, "what are you doing?
Why don't you go for help?"

Ernest had by this time reached a narrow ledge of rock
just above the waterline. I noticed that he was carrying
something over his arm.

"It would take too long," he shouted. "By the time I got
to the Cove and a boat could row back here, you'd be
drowned. Laddie and I will save you. Is there anything there
you can tie a rope to? I've a coil of rope here that I think

will be long enough to reach you. I've been down to the Cove and Alec Martin sent it up to your uncle."

I looked about me: a smooth, round hole had been worn clean through a thin part of the apex of the rock.

"I could fasten the rope if I had it!" I called. "But how can you get it to me?"

For answer Ernest tied a bit of driftwood to the rope and put it into Laddie's mouth. The next minute the dog was swimming out to me. As soon as he came close I caught the rope. It was just long enough to stretch from shore to rock, allowing for a couple of hitches which Ernest gave around a small boulder on the ledge. I tied my camera case on my head by means of some string I found in my pocket, then I slipped into the water and, holding to the rope, went hand over hand to the shore with Laddie swimming beside me. Ernest held on to the shoreward end of the rope like grim death, a task that was no light one for his small arms. When I finally scrambled up beside him, his face was dripping with perspiration and he trembled like a leaf.

"Ern you are a brick!" I exclaimed. "You've saved my life!"

"No, it was Laddie," said Ernest, refusing to take any credit at all.

We hurried home and arrived at Uncle Richard's about ten, just as they were going to bed. When Uncle Richard heard what had happened, he turned very pale. Aunt Kate got me out of my wet clothes as quickly as possible, put me away to bed in hot blankets and dosed me with ginger tea. I slept like a top and felt none the worse for my experience the next morning.

At the breakfast table Uncle Richard scarcely spoke. But, just as we finished, he said abruptly to Ernest, "I'm not going to sell Laddie. You and the dog saved Ned's life between you, and no dog who helped do that is ever going to be sold by me. Henceforth he belongs to you. I give him to you for your very own."

"Oh, Mr. Lawson!" said Ernest, with shining eyes.

I never saw a boy look so happy. As for Laddie, who was sitting beside him with his shaggy head on Ernest's knee, I really believe the dog understood, too. The look in his eyes was almost human. Uncle Richard leaned over and patted him.

"Good dog!" he said. "Good dog!"

AFTER YOU READ

Use story knowledge

Were you surprised about how the story ended? Explain why or why not. How important was the setting to the story? Review your list of story features. Would you add anything after reading this story?

In This Place

In this unit, you have read stories and poems written by Canadian authors that take place in different settings and different times in Canada. Now it is your turn to choose a setting for a poem and story of your own.

▶ Before You Begin

Choose the place you'd like to write about in a poem and use as a setting for a story. Ask yourself these questions:

- Who will read my poem and story?
- What kind of setting do I want to create—funny, scary, unusual, beautiful?
- What kind of story can take place in the setting I have chosen?

Choose a Setting

- a place you've visited
- a place you've read about or heard about
- a place you've imagined

- What emotions do I want my readers to feel?
- What words can I use to make my readers see, hear, taste, or feel what I describe?

Remember, setting is also about time. Will your story take place in the past, present, or future?

Here is a sample of the web Kai Wei made of words and phrases to describe a computer room.

Kaiwei Gan
甘鎧珠

- Sending a postcard on the computer
- Sound of the mouse clicking
- love to send e-mail to friends and relatives
- The computer room
- go on the Internet
- go to my favourite websites
- Try out new CD-Roms

▶ Your First Draft of a Poem

Write a poem using the setting you chose.

1 **Think about the features of your setting.**
- Decide whether it will take place in a country setting or a city setting.
- Decide whether it will take place in Canada or in some other country.
- Decide whether it will be a real or imaginary setting, inside or outside.

2 **Choose the form of your poem.**

3 **Make a word sketch of your poem.**
- Jot down the words or phrases that describe the setting you chose.
- This rough sketch of your poem should create a complete picture of your setting in your mind as you read.

4 **Organize your words and phrases.**
- The words and phrases should follow the form of your poem.
- Make sure that your words and phrases are descriptive and clear.

5 **Write a title for your poem.**
- Your title should also tell something about the setting you chose.

Kai Wei decided to write a haiku poem.

> Haiku
>
> The computer room,
> Sending mail, sending postcards
> Makes me feel happy.

Forms of Poetry
- ▶ a haiku
- ▶ a concrete poem
- ▶ a rhyming poem
- ▶ a free-verse poem

Try This!
Draw or paint a picture of the setting you described in your poem. If you can't create a complete picture, you might want to add more detail to your work.

► Your First Draft of a Story

Write a story about the setting in your poem.

1 **Think about something interesting that might happen in the setting you chose.**

- Reread your poem and ask yourself:
  - ► What kind of story might happen here?
  - ► What characters would you meet here?
  - ► What problems might they encounter?
  - ► How could they try to solve them?
  - ► What would be an interesting ending?

Kinds of Stories

Mystery

Adventure

Folktale

Fable

Historical

Science Fiction

2 **Make a storyboard.**

- Plan the beginning, middle, and end of your story. Jot down some interesting language from your poem to help you get started.

Remember, it is always helpful to plan what you will write by using a storyboard, a flow chart, or another planning tool.

Kai Wei decided to write an adventure story about her encounter with an alien in the computer room. Here is the first part of her draft.

> The Alien
>
> One rainy day at home in the computer room, I was kind of excited because I was on the last level of a game called 'centipede.' I was about to win the game when suddenly the ground started to shake. I thought there was an earthquake. Then the lights began to blink. Everything was falling apart. Only the computer screen stayed really still. Next the computer turned into different colours.

▶ Put It All Together

Here are some ways you might present your poem and story.

- Create a special folder and include illustrations.
- Put your poem and story on your school's web site. (You could organize a class collection!)
- Create a class bulletin board.

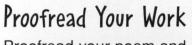

Proofread Your Work

Proofread your poem and story carefully to make sure

- your spelling is correct
- you have included punctuation where you want your reader to pause or at the end of a sentence
- names, place names, and the first word in each sentence are capitalized

Revise and Edit

Polish the language in your poem and make sure your readers can imagine your setting.

- Are your words clear and descriptive?
- Should you add more detail?
- Are there parts that don't fit in your poem?

Rearrange lines and words until the poem seems "right" to you.

■ ■ ■

Look for ways to improve your story.

- Did you create an opening sentence that will hook your reader?
- Is there enough action?
- Are there enough descriptive words, phrases, and different kinds of sentences?

Think about Your Learning

In your poem and story:

- Do your readers have a clear picture of the setting, including the place and time of the story?
- Have you used words and expressions that create powerful word pictures?
- Do your poem and story create a mood or feeling for the reader?
- Did you follow the format for your poem?
- Would dialogue help your story?
- Does your story begin with an interesting problem or situation for the character?
- Does your story ending solve the problem or situation?

ACKNOWLEDGMENTS

Permission to reprint copyrighted material is gratefully acknowledged. Every effort has been made to trace ownership of all copyrighted material and to secure permission from copyright holders. In the event of any question arising as to the use of any material, we will be pleased to make the necessary corrections in future printings.

Photographs
Cover: courtesy of the Canadian Museum of Civilization/Musée Canadien Des Civilisations–S8910839-K89-856; pp. 57-58 courtesy of Arctic Winter Games International Committee/Tom Alvarez; p. 59 Toronto Star/C. McConnell; pp. 60-61 courtesy of Heather McIvor/Jesse Ketchum Public School; p. 68 (left) © Robert Holmes/Corbis, (middle) © E. Hunter/NWP; p. 69 (left) courtesy of the National Capital Commission, (middle) © Peter Dodenhoff/The Canadian Tourism Commission, (top) © Corel Corporation, (top right) © First Light, (bottom right) © Corel Corporation; p. 71 AP/Canapress; p. 72 © Chad Slattery; p. 73 (left) © Corel Corporation, (top and bottom right) © Tim Sheridan/Internet Center for Sand; p. 75 Dave Starrett; p. 76 © Acme Photographic/Beneteau; pp. 77-79 courtesy of Kim Storey; p. 80 courtesy of Douglas Cardinal, Architect; p. 81 (top and middle) courtesy of the National Capital Commission, (bottom) © Mike Pinder/The Canadian Tourism Commission; p. 82 © Todd Eberle/Sygma/Magma Photo News; p. 83 courtesy of Frank O. Gehry & Associates; pp. 97-98 Dave Starrett; pp. 110-111 © Boily Photographers; p. 112 © John Sylvester Photography; p. 114 (left) courtesy of CUQ–Communications, (right) courtesy of The Canadian Tourism Commission; p. 115 Tourism New Brunswick Photo

Illustrations
Cover: Todd Ryoji; pp. 6-7 Steve Attoe; pp. 7-8 Sean Dawdy; pp. 11-15 copyright © 1993 by Steven Kellogg; pp. 18-19, 21 Odile Ouellet; pp. 22-23 Don Kilby; pp. 25-26 Carmelo Blandino; pp. 29, 31-34 Paul Morin; pp. 36-37, 39, 41, 43-45 James Ransome; pp. 47-48, 50, 53, 55 Tadeusz Majewski; p. 58 courtesy of the Arctic Winter Games International Committee; pp. 62-63 Annouchka Galouchko; pp. 64-67 Jun Park; pp. 68-69 Dave MacKay; pp. 77-78 courtesy of Kim Storey; pp. 84-95 Anne Stanley; pp. 101-107 Steve Attoe; pp. 108-109, 113 Bart Vallecoccia; p. 114 Allan Moon; p. 115 Tina Holdcroft; p. 116 Marc Mongeau; pp. 118-121 Jun Park; pp. 122-123 Peter Yundt; p. 125 courtesy of Wing Sham Leung, Ontario; p. 127 courtesy of Marciela Quirola, Ontario; p. 128 courtesy of Bonnie Tang, British Columbia; p. 129 courtesy of Hemon Huang, Ontario; pp. 131-132, 135 Paul Zwolak; pp. 137-138, 140-141 Daphne McCormack; pp. 142-145, 147, 149, 151 Murray Kimber; pp. 152-153 Joe Biafore; pp. 154-156 Ludmila Zeman; pp. 159-160, 163, 165, 167-168 Robert Johannsen; pp. 170 Marion Stuck; p. 171 (top) Barbara Spurll, (bottom) Tracey Wood; p. 172 (top) Nick Vitacco, (bottom) Sue Denti; p. 173 Robert Johannsen; p. 174 From "My Heart Soars© by Chief Dan George and Helmut Hirnschall. Hancock House, 19313 Zero Avenue, Surrey, B.C. Canada V4P 1M7; p. 175 Jane Kurisu; pp. 177-178, 180, 181, 183-185 Paul McCusker; pp. 186-189 Jun Park

Text
"We Are Plooters" by Jack Prelutsky. Copyright © Jack Prelutsky. Reprinted by permission of the author. "The Last Days of the Giddywit" by Natalie Babbitt. From THE BIG BOOK FOR OUR PLANET published by Dutton Children's Books. Reprinted by permission of the author. "The Earth Game" by Pam Conrad. Copyright © 1993 Pam Conrad. Originally published in THE BIG BOOK FOR OUR PLANET